What other are sayin the *Fix Her Upper* books:

"Kick back in your real-life mess and enjoy this fun reminder that The Master Builder is constantly remaking us."

~Anita Renfroe, comedian and author

"I promise you'll laugh while you learn about the beauty of a renovated life."

~Jill Savage, author of *No More Perfect Moms*

"Beth and Rhonda guide you through your own DIY project with the tools you need: Hope with a giant bucket of grace."

~Kathi Lipp, best-selling author of *The Husband Project* and *Clutter Free*

"I love the down-to-earth way Rhonda and Beth bring scriptural truths to real life for us."

~Deborah M. Coty, award-winning author of the *Too Blessed to be Stressed* series

"You'll fall off your chair laughing while finding tips for a reno-job on your life."

~Carole Kent, national speaker and author of *He Holds My Hand*

"If you're feeling rundown, overlooked, and in desperate need of someone to help you see your potential, my friends Beth and Rhonda have a message for you."

~Glynnis Whitwer, author, Doing Busy Better, Exec. Dir. Of Communications, Proverbs 31 Ministries

About the Fix Her Upper books
from Beth Duewel and Rhonda Rhea

Fix Her Upper
Hope and Laughter Through a God-Renovated Life

90-Day Fix Her Upper
Devotional

Fix Her Upper
Reclaim your Happy Space

fix her upper
CHRISTMAS

A Fix Her Upper Christmas

Beth Duewel and Rhonda Rhea

Bold Vision Books
PO Box 2011
Friendswood, Texas 77549

Dedication

In memory of our mamas,

Nancy and Camille,

who orchestrated the happiest fix-her-upper
Christmases on a dime
and wrapped each moment in love and giggles.

Table of Contents

Chapter 1

Have Yourself a Fix Her Upper Christmas ADVENT-ure

Beth and Rhonda

"No wonder my heart is glad, and my tongue shouts his praises! My body rests in hope. You have shown me the way of life, and you will fill me with the joy of your presence"
(Acts 2:26, 28 NLT).

So did anyone else come up with a theme word for last year? Our words were *excellence* (Beth), and *rest* (Rhonda). Put those two together and you have the best nap ever!

We've read several articles that claim naps are life changing. Alertness altering. Energy boosting. Research makes it sound like rest can modify emotional gravity. Even align stars. For sure, star alignment is an unexpected and divine intervention by God. Rest too. Divine. So you thought you were just catching some Z's? No way. Your naps are stringing stars.

But we don't need research to tell us that God's arranged rest is less about sleep and more about refreshment. That His renewal shifts galaxies and leads us to life—life that is full of inexhaustible adventure.

As Fix-Her-Uppers though, we recognize we haven't arrived and wonder at what we have yet to discover. And we're super excited you're on this ADVENT-ure with us. An adventure where we can refresh, anticipate, and wonder at the joy Jesus brings to Christmas. Plus we'll get to celebrate anew with you the true reason we rejoice. Consider strategies for taking those elusive long, snoozy naps. Move planets. That sorta thing.

This new season is a chance to reset our souls and rise above chaos. Talk about emotional gravity. Our mood lifts as we open the gift of Jesus. And there is absolutely no lighter feeling than a fixed focus on Him.

Although we may not be certain of everything, we can be sure of this: the best adventure excites the hope of what's ahead: God's glorious work in progress. Paul reminds us, "For we are his workmanship, created in Christ Jesus for good works, which God prepared beforehand, that we should walk in them" (Ephesians 2:10).

Ready, Set … Restart!

You can read Ephesians 2:10 a million times, and the possibilities will still restart our hope. We are encouraged to enjoy what God creates. Flourish in what He perfects. And rest while He prepares. This is good news for us. Because with all the works "God prepared beforehand," there's simply no need to run or get huffy through the holidays. Many people missed Jesus' birth because they weren't watching for the right kind of king. We don't want to miss any rest because we're busy and searching for the wrong kind of Christmas.

Our perspective on our adventure is as important as our focal point. A fixed focus on the wrong things can certainly tire a soul out. Ironic too, that in Fix-Her-Upper fashion, rustic modern is so many designers' dream décor this year. Because in our modern right-now, amid the hustle and bustle, we can suffer spiritual wear and tear and land heavy on the rustic worn-out without even trying.

But sisters, we can rest.

Our souls are a work in progress. Spiritual rest readies us for the day-to-day work God is doing. Authentic joy is shaped more from the lovely, sometimes ordinary moments when we welcome and nurture that work and find gratitude in it. Rest assured, God loves the handiwork He created (you), and He waits with the excellent respite you soul-deep need.

Let's confess that sometimes it can be a challenge to rest excellently. All too often, we count down the days 'till Christmas by DIY to-dos and decorating redos. We design degrees of urgency to every task. Gather boxes from the basement. Tree-age. Set goals, set dates, set the table for more guests. We're tested with the ability to fix it all. But Christmas isn't about chaos.

Just as Advent prepares our hearts for the hope, love, joy, peace, and the celebration of Jesus' birth—rest prepares us to wait with assurance. It "aligns" our hearts to hover above chaos and settle into joy. To revel in the sacred of the season. Maybe even to take a few unexpected moments to relax.

Get Set for ADVENT-ture

Granted, rest can seem like an inconvenient interruption from more—more goals, more fun, and more time (which we never seem to have enough of). But the internal tug to do more leaves us sighing as we stuff, maybe over stuff, the stockings. We (Beth and Rhonda) will be the first to admit, we can pursue more instead of allowing God to lead us to rest.

This season, we are determined to remember that we're human, preparing our hearts and setting our sights on the abundant more of what God has in store. Which may even involve a kind of less than what we had planned.

We might all be surprised to discover that a slower season isn't as much an encouragement from God to "stay still," but an ADVENT-ure type promise to, "just wait and see what's coming!"

In fact, Paul encourages us to, "Set your minds on things above, not on earthly things" (Colossians 3:2). It's when we set our minds on elevated matters that we find the greatest refreshment and the sweetest surprises all around. It doesn't mean we ignore earthly concerns, or that we don't enjoy them either. In placing our hopes higher, we can find the best rest. Really, what woman isn't up for a satisfying, restful nap? Jesus—the genuine gift of the season—is our real respite in every demo day. The miracle of ease.

There's far more to life for us. Far more that waits ahead. When we have a relationship with Jesus, we are residents of a high heaven! Can you imagine? What a rest-worthy, star-aligned thing to remember.

Our greatest hopes and fears rise and fall on whether we see God's faithfulness in the past and believe He has good planned for our future. And He does.

Be Prepared to Power Nap!

Want an adventure? Dwell and delight in the celebration of the one who came—and who will come again. And while you're thinking about what happened 2,000 years ago, you can praise Jesus for 2,000 more. Also, anticipate some new. New peace in problems. New love for others. New hope for today. New delight for tomorrow. Whatever new you might be looking forward to in this season, there's even more to anticipate.

"Behold, I make all things new" (Revelation 21:5). This is 110% transformation all the time. Talk about stringing stars and moving planets. God is always at work. And someday He will renovate His whole creation—heaven and earth. His big reveal is all part of a beautiful, supernatural surprise.

The idea of a new adventure in the middle of Christmas commotion might seem overwhelming. It doesn't have to be. The eternal celebration Jesus brought to the world—the joy, the peace, the hope—keeps us watching and looking forward to this:

"In peace I will both lie down and sleep; for you alone, O Lord, make me dwell in safety" (Psalm 4:8). This verse is like being *told* to take a nap. Well, okay! These can happen safely morning or midday. Doesn't matter. Let's let our faith rest right there, because truth tells us we can lie down in peace and wake up to the calm and bright of Christmas.

It's because God's love is based on the unchangeable that our hope is based on the unchangeable story that God has come near. "Behold, the virgin shall conceive and bear a son, and they shall call his name Immanuel (which means God with us)" (Matthew 1:23). Built to last, Christmas hope stands on the foundational power of this truth: we are not alone.

While you intend to give this season, work as hard to receive the truth in these promises. Even harder to rest in them. The world waited; Jesus came. Let's live the Advent and embrace the adventure. God moves planets. Strings stars. We can certainly depend on Him to handle the REST. Talk about an excellent power nap. *Ahhh.*

Father, keep me rested and refreshed in You. You are my greatest adventure. Even in the busiest moments, may I have nothing but Your renovating rest this Christmas. Amen.

Chapter 2

When Your Tinsel Is in a Tangle
(Your Lights, Too—In a Tangle)

Beth

"In Him was life, and the life was the light of men. The light shines in the darkness, and the darkness has not overcome it"
(John 1:4-5).

'Twas the first week of December, and all through the land
Not a house was without them, and with receipt in her hand,
"Forty dollars for lights?!" Ah, but they're all the thing;
It's a small price, she thought, *for heaven on a string.*

And that's how it all started.

I'd spotted the must-haves while Jerry and I drove the kids around town to look at Christmas displays. No joke. Icicle lights glistened from *every* house like shiny pairs of dangly earrings.

I poked the car window.

"Oh my gosh," I wheezed. "Wouldn't our eaves look perfect wearing those, honey?"

While I was dazzled by the potential of a million tiny lights, my poor husband knew what waited ahead. Okay, maybe I've had some other *bright* ideas. Like "Let's renovate the basement…" Or "Build a tiny house (in the basement)…" Or "Find an 1890's barn somewhere to refurbish and then use the wood—in the basement!" But this idea to dress every square inch of house with new-fad icicle lights? It was golden. Sparkly bling on a string, twinkling perfection. And it didn't even involve the word "basement." How could my husband resist?

I raved. Jerry blocked me with reason. I enthused. He said things in capital letters with his eyes. Two blocks in and the kids chimed in with *Oohh's* and *Aahh's*. I think Jerry mouthed *Help!* to the cars that drove past us. All-the-way enamored, I continued staring at the shiny houses; so I can't say for sure.

Testy Tangles

I think there's a reason sparkle and Christmas go together so fabulously, and I'd (eventually) convinced Jerry to find out what it was.

Never mind that we knocked real icicles off the gutters to hang fake ones instead. Never mind that it took 260 attempts to stick/clip/glue the tinsley strands to the gutters. Never mind I'd added one more thing on a long *string* of to-dos. Or that the house glowed like day at night! Still, I thought, *What about Christmas decorations really says subtle, anyway?* Besides, the tiny bulbs had already been forced from their perfect packages. We'd go big—at home.

Until the lights went out three days later.

My husband was quick to fix it, and our lights lit merry and bright once again. Four days later though, the luminescent beams totally lost their bling. Not only were the lights horizontally tangly—

but vertically tangly too. With Christmas lights testy, all the hype was gone. I'm ashamed to say I got my tinsel in such a tangle over, of all things, Christmas decorations.

I'm not ashamed to say I read the WARNING label on the box—which basically instructed:

These lights are overrated and prone to burn out. They tangle like your daughter's hair in the pool. They blow over, on top of, and off your house. Sorry, if you're disappointed. I assure you; you are not alone.

Then, the last cautionary words:

Keep them out of inclement weather.

Come on. It's never *not* inclement weather in Ohio.

Detangled

Despite the house adornment disaster, I maintained the possibility that a home wrapped in lights could illuminate out-and-out joy. Even outshine the tangles in life. And it can. I had a vision of what I wanted Christmas to be, shiny and perfectly bright, but that December my glistening ideal unplugged with my father's diagnosis of Alzheimer's. *Moody* and bright—Christmas didn't look, feel, or happen at all like I'd envisioned. But you know what did happen?

Christmas!

Christmas arrived and was more wonderful and beautiful and memorable than in years past. It came without fanfare or fuss. And fewer fuses and fixes meant more time to enjoy each other. To focus. To pray. Christmas was shiniest that year, all because we centered on the incandescence of Jesus' joy.

Maybe, like me, you're excited about the hope the holiday holds. Because while a few dark days can try to tie our thrill up in knots, our shiny reason to celebrate has never burned brighter.

Although I'll admit, two lights try to sparkle in this world: my own idea of larger-than-life, perfect light, and the One who actually *is* that larger-than-life, perfect light.

Honestly, it's good when life loses some of its luster. It seems when we let things "outshine" they light up spaces not really intended for them. Perfect joy can be so easily misinterpreted. A close but distant mix of both the light of elation and the shadow of sorrow, joy isn't flashy or showy. But girl, can it light up a room!

Temporary Tinsel Tangles Too

You can believe life provides plenty of "shiny" to distract us. Our finger hits the car window as our heartstrings wrap around our vision of right. But temporary tinsel tangles, too. God knows we can't shove the expectations of this life into a God-sized space. He understands that it's impossible to straighten out our faith without Him. But also. That we continue to DIY try.

Which is exactly why I'm so taken by the easy gift of Christmas. The subtle confidence of it. In fact, Isaiah addressed completeness and flawlessness when he talked about what Jesus' kingdom accomplished.

"Of the greatness of his government and peace there will be no end. He will reign on David's throne and over his kingdom, establishing and upholding it with justice and righteousness from that time and forever. The zeal of the Lord Almighty will accomplish this" (Isaiah 9:7 NIV). We need this great hope. Jesus' holiness outshines our sin, and His blinding love invites us into relationship despite it. Forever. What shiny relief. The light and promise of Christ's reign brings merry with it. Grace too, as God's love accomplished what we cannot: perfection.

Infinity Lights? That's Right!

I confess that sometimes my big ideas try to capture the spotlight, even the Christmas light. But God's plan for everlasting joy is too brightly illuminated to miss.

"But when the fullness of the time had come, God sent forth His Son, born of woman, born under the law, to redeem those who were under the Law, so that we might receive adoption as sons" (Galatians 4: 4-5). The certainty of Jesus as our Redeemer can untangle our lives. There's no situation, circumstance, or fear so dark that God's great hope can't permeate. Why?

Because Christmas is the truth and promise of a relationship with the One whose light shines the brightest. There is no need to get our tinsel in a tangle. With our spotlight on Jesus, we can have the perfect confidence that Christmas brings.

Also. *Maybe, perhaps, possibly* the new rope lights out this year, because … "Honey, can't you just see those hanging on our house?!"

Father, I am prone to wander, and prone to desire for this life to be perfect. When I know You, it should show in the overflow of my heart. It should light up dark corners of my heart with joy and peace and the contentment of believing You are a God of grace. Light the way from my heart, to my words, to my ideas and days. Make Your infinite hope and light visible and present in me. Everything in my life will reveal its imperfection. But in the fullness of time, You came to save. What a perfect plan, Jesus. What perfect love. What infinite light. Amen.

The Thrill of Hope from Rhonda

Anybody else asking with us why it would be recommended that we not use outside lights … for the outside? Outside lights! How many Midwesterners have not experienced at least a day or two of inclement weather in a holiday season? Is that even possible? Seems rather "outside" sensible reason, to me.

Yet even there, there's "gracing the gap" as Beth described it. What a great reminder that God has fixed our hearts through Christ. His fix for our inside shines its way to the outside. In every kind of weather. Thank You, Father!

Chapter 3

Chocolate Covered Christmas

Rhonda

"Now the birth of Jesus Christ took place in this way. When his mother Mary had been betrothed to Joseph, before they came together she was found to be with child from the Holy Spirit. And her husband Joseph, being a just man and unwilling to put her to shame, resolved to divorce her quietly. But as he considered these things, behold, an angel of the Lord appeared to him in a dream, saying, "Joseph, son of David, do not fear to take Mary as your wife, for that which is conceived in her is from the Holy Spirit. She will bear a son, and you shall call his name Jesus, for he will save his people from their sins"
(Matthew 1:18-21).

Anytime something breaks around the house at Christmas time, you should always glue it back together with melted chocolate. DIY and done!

If I had a nickel for every time I've said no to someone offering me something uber chocolate covered from their well-constructed tower of fudgy Christmas party delights … well, I would still have zero nickels. Could I possibly have less than zero nickels? And does anyone ever say no to some of that chocolate? I've seen a lot of chocolate towers. Practically a castle's worth of them. Still no nickels.

I wonder if there's anything we won't cover with fudge during the holidays. Not that I'm complaining. I try not to encourage it, but I seem to have to. I've told my closest choco-loving friends that I would've named one of our children Ghirardelli if my husband would've let me. Fannie Mae? That name was in the running too. Godiva? Okay, that one seemed wrong, even to me. But I was still strongly considering "Whitman" for one of the boys. I'm a long-time respecter of all things chocolate-covered. My favorite is when people just give up the silly pretense and start covering *chocolate* with chocolate.

I feel like people who say that diamonds are a girl's best friend don't really understand how much we like chocolate chips.

What We Really Want

I understand that you can't really go by me as far as what women want. All of us—women, men, children, teens—we all tend to want whatever is wrong for us. That off-kilter "wanter" came with the curse of sin.

That prompts me to love Christmas all the more. Love it more than chocolate on chocolate on chocolate. Christmas is the concentrated, celebrative reminder that Jesus came to deal with the sin curse we were powerless to break. Because He paid in full with His own blood what was needed to provide the remedy for sin, He gives us His own righteousness and a right and tight relationship with a holy God. He makes us new. And with that newness comes a new way of wanting. Paul said, "For it is God who works in you, both to will and to work for his good pleasure" (Philippians 2:13).

The Amplified Version of the Bible expands on the passage this way. "For it is not your strength, but it is God who is effectively at work in you, both to will and to work [that is, strengthening, energizing, and creating in you're the longing and the ability to fulfill your purpose] for His good pleasure." He gives us the ability, the strength, and the energy to do good—and then, by His strength, He gives us the longing, the will, the *desire* to do it. He's got us covered in every perfect way, all the way to the soul.

There's nothing more delicious in this existence than accomplishing God's purposes in our lives and bringing our Creator "good pleasure." It's what we were made for.

The Dreamiest Gift

I think Joseph was a man who wanted to accomplish the purposes of God in His life. What a kick in the gut it must've been for him when he found that the girl he was to marry was pregnant with a child that wasn't his. Under Jewish law, he had every right to make Mary's humiliation public and have her stoned. But Matthew 1:19 tells us that Joseph was a "just man."

I picture a heartbroken Joseph tossing and turning, then slipping off into a troubled sleep. But what a wake-up call! It was a stunning message from an angel in a dream. The angel told Joseph that it was okay to take Mary as his wife and that her baby was conceived by the Holy Spirit. He would be the Savior!

So what did Joseph do? "When Joseph woke from sleep, he did as the angel of the Lord commanded him" (Matthew 1:24). He got up and did exactly as he was told. I wonder if he ever even stopped to think about what he "wanted" to do. I wouldn't be the least bit surprised to find out that God had already tweaked his "wanter." Joseph wanted to honor God's plan. I believe He wanted to honor God's plan even before he knew how grand and glorious that plan would be.

The Happiest Ending—that Never Ends

Because Joseph followed God, he got to witness His bigger purpose up close and personal. "Immanuel." "God with us" (vs.23).

Three powerful words that rocked history. "God with us." That's really all I want for Christmas, too. Celebrating the redemption we have in Him—the redemption that is our eternal, most blessed covering—honest and truly, that's enough for me.

Though if you insist on getting me a gift anyway, I don't suppose I should argue. Let the chips fall where they may. You know I mean chocolate chips, right?

> *O Lord, by Your Spirit, help us ignore every empty want, and ever want what You want. Strengthen and enable us to get up and take the first steps of following Your direction before we even know Your plan. Let us respond to You with unhesitating, unrestrained, all-with-abandon obedience.*

Merry and Bright from Beth

I love this chapter so much I want to eat it. Just today I had to use superglue to fix a plate and thought, *If only this was chocolate; I'd be licking my fingers instead of prying them apart.* Such a great reminder that God's "good pleasure" is more but different than I've ever imagined. Sometimes it's painful. Other times, delicious. But I look back on those times I've prayed, *God please fix this,* only to realize my idea of "broken" was the more beautiful whole. Infertility. Illness. Shatters and shards. May God use His fixes to forever lead us to Him.

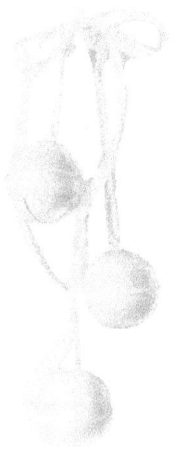

Chapter 4

Let's Unwrap the Gift

Beth

"Thanks be to God for this inexpressible gift!"
(2 Corinthians 9:15).

One Christmas we didn't get a Christmas list from our son. We got an idea.

He wanted one thing: a minibike. No more toy trucks. Tweenage boys want engines, keys, and tires that go flat. According to the pre-Christmas convos my son and I had, they *need* these things, and "Isn't this the best idea, Mom?"

Josh would lead off with, "Mom, I really don't want a lot of *stuff* for Christmas." His plan? Qualitative vs. quantitative. You know, with all the money we were saving on all the "stuff" he was not asking for, we could buy the one big "stuff" he really wanted.

I could already tell by the twinkle lights in my husband's eyes…our son would get stuff. By which I mean my husband would figure out a way to stuff a miniature motorcycle down our fireplace. Of course we wanted it to be reasonably priced. Unfortunately, the reasonable price showed up only a week before Christmas in an ad that read, "needs some work."

Ooooh a restoration project, I thought. But then "needs work" turned into "an overhaul," which turned into "new everything." Plus—a paint job. A total redo.

Per usual for our parent-present-projects, the fixing up required 10 cans of Christmas Red paint and 20 trips to the store. Also, the garage floor took a hard hit of over spray. It's probably no surprise that, all these years later, the cement still shows a minibike imprint of the love we gave away in 2006. What can I say? We spray.

Oh, NO, HO, HO!

A commiseratory kudos to the parents who, like Jerry and me, burn the midnight oils—not in peppermint or frankincense, but in oil-based paint. Perhaps like us you've come to realize this particular paint takes a year to dry. Two to stop smelling. I do admire you.

Mostly because … *You survived!*

Moreover—you stayed up all night assembling the Christmas gift, mumbling about the Christmas gift, and asphyxiating yourself over the Christmas gift, and still you lived to tell about it on Christmas Day. Well, you probably didn't really tell about it. More like you whisper-yelled with your spouse and then opened all the windows to eradicate the fumes, which is important. Very responsible.

It also makes for a colder—but more *alive*—Christmas morning.

The fun doesn't stop there.

What you do next is always the same: you gather the kids to try all the gifts out, right? I mean, you almost died fixing it up, you might as well see them take a joy ride on it. And by "ride" I mean one daughter does a wheelie before landing in the tree row, and another child runs into the doghouse, leaving a red paint scuff on the roof. BAM! At least it matches the garage floor now. I love a good color scheme.

Seems surviving Christmas is more than just a goal of ours. It. Is. Our. Life's. Work. Really, what does Christmas think we are? Invincible? It's surprising how much grit and passion we pour into gift giving. Without hesitation, we throw ourselves in. We do. We redo. All the "stuff" can overwhelm.

Thriving at Christmas

This is our fourth Fix Her Upper book. Is it clear by now that I'm a doer? I think it's part of human nature to want to fix things, make things right. For example, nothing rattles me more than being caught off guard. When my crisis mode is activated, I do the weird thing and clean. Or work feverishly on a project. Any major issue pops up unexpectedly, and my inner Martha comes out. I fuss. I fret. I scrub the surface off of all the countertops.

For example, when Jerry and I struggled with infertility I scraped five layers of wallpaper off the walls of our first fixer upper. And liked it. To reiterate what a crazy train that was, what acrylic nails I didn't wear down while scraping and rubbing and peeling wallpaper off during the day … *ehhh* … I bit off at night! *Nervous energy, people!*

Then one night Jerry woke up.

"Beth, is that you crunching? Are you biting your fake nails?" "Uhhh, yes." After that I heard his eyes roll (because it was a really loud roll). And when I say things like fruitcake tastes like acrylic nails, I know he knows that I know. It's not a figure of speech. I've nailed it.

My point is, we can inundate ourselves with uncertainty, fear, and doubt. When we fretfully rearrange our world, scrub the counters, and chew the nails (or when we turn service into survival), it's as if we are trying to qualify the love and loving indulgence God wants to give. Believe me, sometimes we try to substitute task for trust, calculate quantity over quality, and alternate fixes for faith. I know you know that I know how easy it is to consider God's love as linear.

But like a parent to a child—God's love makes no sense.

The Glorious Giver

We parents want to give our children good gifts (albeit sometimes compulsively, neurotically, and ridiculously). But hey, we give.

A lot of the time parents give lavishly, abundantly, and generously to their children all while risking asphyxiation. Our love paints with the widest brush. So how much more does our Father want to give to us? Generously? Sacrificially?

"If you then, who are evil, know how to give good gifts to your children, how much more will your Father who is in heaven give good things to those who ask him!" (Matthew 7:11). We see that it's wonderful to give. But also, glorious to give up.

The more time I spend with God in prayer, and the more frequently I unwrap His truth, the more excited I am to accept the "good things" He has planned. Christmastime can be holy (all about Jesus) and set apart. Or it can feel like the "stuff" of sheer survival. Allowing ourselves to be loved by God, trying less and leaning more, this, this is the greatest gift of Christmas. To receive.

The Gracious Receiver

Not accepting the great gift of Jesus at Christmas is living like the Israelite's who were "not able to enter [The Promised Land] because of their unbelief" (Hebrews 3:19 NIV). The Israelites had the good news of the Promised Land just steps away, but they never entered in.

I love the truth of this passage until I don't. Sometimes it's difficult to believe God has such extravagant gifts waiting just beyond the next trial, crisis, or uncertainty. How about we unwrap the trust that believes that what waits for us is good?

I must admit, the undeserved kindness of the Lord is greater than I can begin to understand. Yet all these gifts of forgiveness, hope, joy, salvation—they wait. For you. And for me.

So you know how some parents save the best gift for last? I mean, in case someone needs to go to the hospital or something? Well, here it is: Jesus' gift is everlasting and eternal. Harm free. The literal glory of God, He lives. The Old Testament tells us that no man can see God's glory and not die. "'But,' he said, 'You cannot see my face, for man shall not see me and live'" (Exodus 33:20).

Then, in the knowledge of the wonderful gift God would give that first Christmas, He promised, "The glory of the Lord shall be revealed" (Isaiah 40:5a). Jesus is the revelation of God's gift and living glory. The exact imprint of the love He gave on the cross. "He is the radiance and glory of God, and the exact imprint of His nature" (Hebrews 1:3a). Christmas is a day to look back and marvel at all God has gloriously offered. The greatest gift: Himself.

We have a good and generous gift, Girls! Let's open it! And if you're DIYing all the kids' gifts for Christmas this year, well, you may want to open the windows. Every. Single. One. Don't ask me how I know...but I know you know that I know. I just know.

Father, how gracious You are. You are making something beautiful out of my life, out of my broken pieces, out of my issues, and my whole heart's faith. Take this, Lord. My life and my tendency to fix and fret. Take my time. My talent. Give it away as You see fit. Use my humble offering for your highest calling—to love others. Oh, that I may settle in and trust the work You are doing. Help me trust Your generous love. To pass it on. To give forgiveness away. Grace too. Thank You, Father. Amen.

The Thrill of Hope from Rhonda

Some people paint the town red, I hear. Beth and Jerry? The garage floor. And the doghouse. And whatever else the family slammed that machine into. I'll admit right here that not only am I entertained by Beth's doer-fixer-inner-Martha-ness, I love it. I even admire it. Believe it or not, I've seen her get rather "Martha-worky" about getting "Mary-worshippy." I've known her to work hard to make that time with Jesus she talks about in this chapter. I'm praying the Lord will make me more of that excellent Martha-Mary mix like my friend, and that I will work to find space in every day to breathe in His presence. Oh how I do not want to miss this gift.

So I'm taking a breath right now. And after Beth's experience, I'm that much more thankful it's a non-asphyxiating, fume-free breath.

Chapter 5

Don't I Wish

Rhonda

"Hear my cry, O God, listen to my prayer; from the end of the earth I call to you when my heart is faint. Lead me to the rock that is higher than I, for you have been my refuge, a strong tower against the enemy. Let me dwell in your tent forever! Let me take refuge under the shelter of your wings! Selah"
(Psalm 61:1-4).

Ah, Christmas shopping. When you can find yourself completely enveloped in the smell of evergreen. And maybe pepper spray. Does the shopping seem to go on and on for anybody else? And then … on? Then also … on? Anyone else get weary of the crowds and the crazy and the considerable consumerism? How are we going to fixer-upper *that*? I try to prepare myself for all that. Prepare, not pepper. Because I was not the one with the pepper spray. That wasn't me. Though if it was you, I will not judge.

I confess, though, that the seemingly never-ending shopping season is a Santa-sized bag of troubles I've all too often experienced. And I inflicted it on myself. That was me.

When my five kids were little, I remember sometimes feeling my children thought my Christmas list was some sort of magic lamp. Make a wish, rub the list, and POOF! It's under the tree. I might even remember one of them wishing for three more wishes.

Every year I would resolve not to over-shop. Not to get sucked in. Not to be manipulated. I would be very determined ... as I wrote all their "wishes" down on my long shopping list and headed out to the stores. As I headed out, mind you, for the purpose of getting everything on the list. All of it. Like a bit of a mom-chump. Incidentally, just to attempt to be somewhat responsible, I would try to limit myself to five or six hours of shopping per trip, but it usually took about that long just to find a parking spot.

Wishes on Wishes on Wishes

It was the most frazzling time of the year. I have to tell you, I had a few wishes of my own back then. A lot of my wishes were spa related. Then sometimes I'd be almost finished with the shopping when somebody would come up with a new wish. *What?* I wonder how many times I heard myself saying, "How 'bout we have a little less wishing and a little more cleaning your bathroom."

Yeah ... less wishy. More washy.

Then again, who was I to talk about wishy-washy? After all, I was the adult who waffled under the pressure to grant all the desires of all the littles.

In Psalm 27, David wrote about his number one wish. He said, "One thing have I asked of the Lord, that will I seek after" (verse 4). Okay, David. First of all, you're doing it wrong. *One* thing? Just one? Check your list because that's not how we do it.

Wishing for Just This

Then he tells us clearly what the one thing that he really wants is: "that I may dwell in the house of the Lord all the days of my life, to gaze upon the beauty of the Lord and to inquire in his temple" (Psalm 27:4).

The presence of the Lord. To dwell with Him. To see Him. To talk to Him in the place where He dwells. Just to be with Him. That's the one gift that will actually change us. Toys and clothes and treats and "things" will come and go. But the presence of the Lord will make a difference all the way to the soul. It changes a family from the inside out. Oh that we will pepper our days with a consuming desire for His presence.

It's downright embarrassing that I can still so easily get wrapped up in lists and wants, the busyness and the noise and the stuff, and lose sight of who we're celebrating. God coming as a human, knowing He was destined for the cross—it's the most beautiful redemption story. Celebrating His birth in His presence. That makes so much frazzle-free sense. Presence. Not presents. It's a real gift to our children when we get this in the right order—and when we don't waffle.

We can't remind ourselves enough that because of the Real Gift of the Christ of Christmas, God's presence has been made available to each of us. Yes, Christ, our Redeemer, by His sacrifice on the Cross, has given us access to fellowship with our holy God in a remarkable closeness. God Himself, indwelling us. What a miracle.

We never have to shop for this miraculous closeness to God our Father. We don't have to wish for it or work for it. It's real and accessible for every person who has become a follower of the Savior. In every moment we will quiet our hearts and remember the truth—even when we're surrounded by every kind of earthly noise—the quiet presence of the God who indwells us makes life different. Better. Beautiful.

Less Waffling, Less Frazzling

You might be interested to know that I eventually got a better handle on my wishy-washy-"wishy" ways. Yes, more presence. Fewer presents. We implemented a three-gift rule. Jesus got gold, frankincense and myrrh. Even the kids agreed they shouldn't get more gifts than

Jesus. We pared back (though I should probably confess here that I totally rocked out the stockings). Most of the time, I shopped, spent and stressed less. Would you believe the kids did NOT feel less loved?

And it might encourage you to know that this year I did my Christmas shopping early and didn't even need a list. Grown kids and gift cards, thank you very much. Because (tongue planted firmly in cheek) nothing says "love" and "this is how much I'm willing to spend on you" like a gift card.

Father, be my one true consuming desire. Guard my heart and mind even right now, I ask. I don't want to let the temporary distract me from the eternal. How I thank You that You've made it possible through Your Son, Jesus Christ, for me to experience Your presence personally. Real and close and sweet. May the Christmas season make me more aware of the privilege and blessing of Your presence than ever. May Psalm 27:4 continually be my testimony. My mindset and my heart-set: "One thing have I asked of the Lord, that will I seek after: that I may dwell in the house of the Lord all the days of my life, to gaze upon the beauty of the Lord and to inquire in his temple."

Merry and Bright from Beth

Have you ever noticed how merry and bright a room looks after a good declutter? How much larger it seems? Well, I love this larger look as we're encouraged to remember that there is no scarcity with God. Also, that there's no cleaner, fresher, grander place to be than in God's house. Once there—we can only gaze with wonder at who God is. Rhonda, I want to be less wishy and more "watchy." To watch and see God's joy and generosity hold up to all the stuff this Christmas. Forever. Amen.

Chapter 6

Christmas in a K-Cup

Beth

*"Then times of refreshment will come from the presence of
the Lord, and he will again send you Jesus, your appointed
Messiah"*
(Acts 3:20 NLT).

We all have our moments of desperate.
Yesterday was that for me.
My daughter's been on me NOT to waste the coffee K-cups because "Mom, these things are good for another cup of coffee." At the holidays, too, we need to conserve. So when I ran out of caffeine, I left my k-cup nestled in its nest just like Brooklyn said to do. I brewed it through again. Even on the weak side, with lots of creamer, I figured my taste buds would hardly know the lie my mug was telling. But they

knew. By noon I could have chewed on a coffee bean and liked it. The recycled coffee was too weak to do its job. It was...just okay.

Kind of like the holidays for me. I start out strong. In a can-do spirit, I rally all my resolve. Then I do well to take the Christmas lights down by spring. Why would I ever expect to change my world around in such a short season?

So, in full blown holiday zeal I'm determined and think, "The world is my oyster. Or my cup of coffee? This Christmas will be the season for solid effort and do-it-all." Then I throw out all our family's unmatched socks. Like I believe if I can start over with neat pairs I'll be able keep my chaotic world together in kind. Isn't this some kind of ridiculousness? My resolve turns out to be a recycled regimen at best.

Half-Caff

If you're like me, you see the busy begin to brew in November. Sometimes even October. This craziness starts and steeps through to the Christmas bustle.

On top of self-imposed pressure, I recite new lists and resolve to push through on the bright side. I gather more grit. But by December 1, my resolution is over. I'm wearing mismatched socks. At the end of my motivated frenzy—I still feel good about my aspirations—but my joy is weak. My hope? Watered down. My concentration is ½ caff. No whip. I feel a little desperate and out of sorts. I'm just okay.

I feel like a recycled K-cup!

Even the Christmas story can run through our hearts again and again and feel watered-down the more we hear it. But we have this eternal hope: the Spirit never loses its power to change us.

Sometimes the holidays can seem like DIY magnified. I mean, there can be some bold feelings about Christmas, am I right? With the holidays come hard soul-striving, identity-misplacing, and sad-fixing. Or at least trying. Then, when anticipations aren't met, we crash like a k-cup.

The Sorted Truth

I remember my mom feeling this seasonal struggle. Once, after a day of crowds and shopping, she took us kids for ice cream. We were happy and hyper and she asked us not to slurp our ice cream so loud, "Because I just need a quiet minute to sort myself." Now with my own children and stress I'm like, *Ohhhh! And ohhhh ...*

Seems the enemy is ever the captor at Christmastime. When our energy is depleted, we can be easily led to believe we're above his schemes and sways. We trust our grit to get us through. All this, while we're watered-down and walking around with ... well ... ice cream stains on our outfits.

Just the other day, my husband came into my office to say hello. I felt weak, worn out and tired. I had tried all morning to "sort myself." Jerry listened while I bemoaned *everything,* including the chocolate ice cream stains on my pants.

I rambled, "It's like ice cream is dropping from the ceiling. I can't figure it out."

I looked up while my husband leaned in for a closer look, and then began to laugh. He. Could. Not. Stop!

He finally gasped it out, "It's not dripping from the ceiling, honey. It's dripping from your chin. Don't you feel that?" *Well then, there it is.* Sometimes we don't realize the mess our flesh is capable of. We look around and wonder, *How in the world did this happen?* Never realizing we're the source of our own frustrations. It's dripping right off our chins.

Strength, depth, and completeness are dispensed into our souls when we allow our lives to flow through God's truth. We ask. We pray. We are led. Then, when our resolve is gone—when our feelings try to bully us (or when ice cream tricks us)—we'll know exactly what we're up against.

We won't trade our wholeness for this world's halfness. We will have the courage-strength-faith to carry us through.

The Bold-Brewed Promise

Heart and head disconnect? It happens. Slowly sometimes. But it's a self-reliance recycle of the worst kind. Even King Solomon knew the struggle. Scripture reminds us that, "God gave Solomon wisdom and very great insight, and a breath of understanding as measureless as the sand on the seashore…he was wiser than any other man" (1 Kings 4:29-31 NIV). But as we continue to read, we discover that as Solomon grew older, his wives turned his heart "after other gods" (11:4).

The vulnerability of Solomon's struggle can challenge the lie we tell ourselves: that our resolve depends on us, and that our head and heart won't lead us astray. We can believe other falsehoods, too, like … *Coffee will taste as great and strong and vibrant when brewed a second time*! But we are bold-brewed in sin and need the Holy Spirit's help. A latte.

God's Grande Good

So how do we do life at one hundred percent? How do we refresh our resolve, our hope, our joy—when life feels just okay? Take a look at this strength.

"The steadfast love of the Lord never ceases, his mercies never come to an end; they are new every morning; great is your faithfulness (Lamentations 3:22-23).

We can reuse this absolute reminder to "perk" up because God's love never runs out. His mercy doesn't either. This is the promise of calm in uncontrollable chaos. When God's goodness is "new every morning" there is no such life as "just okay."

There is relief. At Christmas and all year round.

Because a huge multitude of angels appeared praising God and saying, "Glory to God in the highest, and on earth peace, good will toward men" (Luke 2:14 KJV). Something miraculous happens when we depend on God's effort to glory over our lives. This verse is literal proof that God has blessed us and shows distinct favor to His own. With Jesus's birth came forgiveness and grace and eternal reconciliation with God. Also. The help of the Holy Spirit. The hope of Jesus at Christmas is the grande-cup of assurance we can consume.

It's not about more can-do spirit, caffeinated drive, determination, or happy in us. Not at Christmas, anyway. Or any time of the year. Our trust needs to brew deeper than our own capabilities. Seriously. It's exhausting trying to slap happy together and find socks that match. And if you've ever struggled with depression around Christmastime—you know the DIY stuff just doesn't work.

So today, friends, we can leap for joy with the bold truth of who God is in us. Also leap for coffee. Although, I had to recycle another K-Cup, so my leaping looks more like a tantrum right now. But still.

Father, we are eager for holiday joy; we embrace it. The family traditions, the gift giving, the excitement, and the thrill of looking forward to the year ahead that You've designed. It's awe-inspiring! But my enthusiasm can run out with the sheer scope of it all. Keep me joyful and alive in Spirit. This year has been a lot, Lord, but the weary world still rejoices! And here I am. Living in Your day of grace. Celebrating in a time of weary. Trusting in Your perfect plan. Help me work harder to press in to You. Your Word will lift me. May my mind seek, my heart long for, and my Spirit follow You. Amen.

The Thrill of Hope from Rhonda

I'm chewing my lip a little right now, trying not to laugh when Beth says she could've chewed on a coffee bean and liked it. Because I remember that time she and I were at a conference together and she ate about three-quarters of a pound of chocolate-covered coffee beans. And then had heart palpitations for like a year. I remember her surprise. "What? Those have a lot of caffeine?" I don't think she slept for three days.

You might be happy to know she has since resolved not to eat those things by the pound. I think we're both asking the Lord to help us make better resolutions this holiday season as well, never allowing the most real message of Christmas to become weak or watered down. May we stay "perky"—energetically enthusiastic in all the right ways.

Chapter 7

The Christmas Feels and the Christmas Fills

Rhonda

*"Then Jesus said to His disciples, 'If anyone wishes to follow
Me [as My disciple], he must deny himself [set aside selfish
interests], and take up his cross [expressing a willingness to
endure whatever may come] and follow Me [believing in Me,
conforming to My example in living and, if need be, suffering
or perhaps dying because of faith in Me]. For whoever wishes
to save his life [in this world] will [eventually] lose it [through
death], but whoever loses his life [in this world] for My sake
will find it [that is, life with Me for all eternity]'"*
(Matthew 16:24-25 AMP).

That Christmas feeling. All year long. Because Christmas movies.
All. Year. Long.

I have a high threshold for the feel-good movies with lots of snow and carols and cookie sprinkles. I watch them all. So when Christmas rolls around for real, I get excited. Christmas movies—at Christmas!

I've seen enough of these movies to know that to experience the season well, you have to fill it with the proper Christmas components. Christmas cookie-baking (spoiler alert: the secret ingredient is love), decorating the tree while singing loud carols (possibly falling off a ladder), ice-skating, brushing something off someone's face, and, of course, making snow angels. We don't always get a good Christmas snow outside of the movies. For the record, dirt angels are not the same. And Christmas laundry could also become a thing.

I had a little trouble last year. Not with the dirt angels, but with the tree-decorating/loud singing part. A dozen extra packages of tinsel and too many extra-loud choruses of "Joy to the World" and I got the worst sore throat. Pretty sure I had tinselitis.

Over-loud, Over-stuffed—Over It!

There's a different kind of loud message around this time of year, though. It's both loud and subtle—and not funny. It's a message to fill the season. Fill it with stuff and stuff it to the max. Fill it with busy and merch and hustle and bustle—and the fullest lists. We've mentioned lists, haven't we? Because we're talking about lists on lists on lists. Fill it with chaos and stress and nary a silent night, much less sleep in heavenly peace.

I'll tell you exactly what I do *not* want my season filled with. Regret. That's what happens when we let our focus drift to the wrong fillings. There's a beautiful filling that happens, however—as weird as it sounds—in the proper emptiness. An appreciation of Christmas, and life itself, blossoms as we fill life with … sacrifice. Fill it with surrender.

As we surrender to Jesus, life is filled with purpose. Jesus said, "If anyone would come after me, let him deny himself and take up his cross daily and follow me. For whoever would save his life will lose it, but whoever loses his life for my sake will save it. For what does it profit a man if he gains the whole world and loses or forfeits himself?" (Luke 9:23-25).

I can fill up with the temporary—money, fame, success, power—whatever this world might offer. Gaining it all. Losing myself.

The ultimate regret. The Message paraphrases part of the passage like this: "Self-help is no help at all. Self-sacrifice is the way, *my* way, to finding yourself, your true self. What good would it do to get everything you want and lose you, the real you?" (THE MESSAGE).

It's not a tough choice. Lose the real me? Or surrender to the Lord, holding nothing back, and go His way. His way is an open door to full life. Joyful. And joy-full.

Get Your Fill

We were never meant to fill ourselves with joy. We weren't built to wrangle purpose out of our existence. Trying it leads to joylessness— and regrets on regrets on regrets.

I think I'll stop right here and sing. Loud.

> *"Joy to the world, the Lord is come*
> *Let earth receive her King"*

Jesus came to bring joy to this world, fully knowing what it would cost Him. What a glorious example of sacrifice. He set aside heaven and His rights as God-King, trading them for suffering—and all for the joy of closeness with us.

We can trust that when He asks us to abandon all and follow Him, He does it with our good in mind. If we let go and grab onto Him, we always find that His plans for us are bigger and better than anything we could've dreamed up. This is a King I can follow without reservation.

That thought fills my heart with singing. Year-round. Though from here on out I might do the actual singing with a little more reservation.

> *Father, thank You for introducing the truest joy into my life*
> *through Your Son, Jesus Christ. At every instance I'm tempted*
> *to trade joy in You for temporary pleasure in "stuff," open my*
> *eyes to Your truth and Your purpose for me. I surrender to You*
> *right now. Fill me with Your presence, Your joy, Your mission*
> *for me. Empower me to follow You, whatever it might cost me.*

May I serve You with complete abandon, regret-free, all by the strength and power of Your Holy Spirit, and all for Your glory. Following You, my King.

Merry and Bright from Beth

So, the first time I tried espresso beans I devoured the entire bag? It was chocolate *and* coffee. And I quickly filled up on the equivalent of no less than but possibly more than ten cups of java. There might be an upside to this much indulgence ... said no one ever. I was a hot mess express...O! At Christmastime too, there is the idea to indulge in O' so many ways. It's great to remember that Luke 2 is about how every prophecy was fulfilled in Jesus. Every full feeling of joy, peace, and love was born with Him. He is the greatest extravagance. *Not espresso beans, Beth.* O' not those!

Chapter 8

The Joy of Missing Out

Beth

*"When you call on me, when you come and pray to me, I'll
listen. When you come looking for me, you'll find me.
Yes, when you get serious about finding me and want it more
than anything else, I'll make sure you won't be disappointed"*
(Jeremiah 29:12-14 The Message).

This world is busy. Christmas? Busier still.

For instance, when I was young, the recently re-popular "elf
on a shelf" just ... sat on the shelf. That's it. A static annual dec-
oration in our home, he sat, he stared, he seemed to be in a type of elf
timeout. Did he do yoga back then? Rock climbing? Snowball fights?
No. As a kid, I had to dust him.

Now apparently, he has to "go" places. He stays super busy.

Because if he doesn't—well, he misses out on Christmas magic and friends and, per his Instagram pictures, games in the laundry room. And hanging out in the laundry room. And sleeping in the laundry room. It's somehow always the laundry room. W*hy?*

Always on the move, you can even wrap the elf in foil and send him to the moon. Help him make snow angels in powdered sugar, or meet up with his friends for coffee. Not kidding. I break more than one bead of sweat watching him stay so busy.

Missing What, Exactly?

I mean, isn't it enough to try to decide whether or not to investigate the loud thump resonating from the upstairs? Now we have to wonder if it's the elf up in the attic causing such a clatter.

When it's time to move the elf, please note I may need a reminder. Between holiday errands last year I had to stop and ask my husband, "What's the name of that woman who works somewhere and does that thing? You know. What?" He knew who it was. Where it was. And that it was our taxes! He. Is. Good. Me? My brain cells tend to stay more sedentary lately. I can't begin to know where I left the elf last. Possibly on the moon. I really don't know.

Each day, we get to decide whether to live like an elf on the edge of somebody's shelf. Teetering and tasking. And I'll even admit to low-grade worrying that I'm not experiencing the same joy as the rest of the world. Or that I won't be invited to make snow angels in powdered sugar, which I totally want to do. Sometimes I worry I'll miss out on the one hundred percent life and the amazement and wonder of Christmas that everyone else enjoys. I still completely know there is no fun to be had in the laundry room. I may feel like a silly elf, but I'm not that far gone.

Finding Freedom

Year to year, holidays can change can't they? But even if this December feels less like my usual way of following the arrows through IKEA with an unexpected need to go back to the towels—my nervous thoughts continue to propel me in the same direction. My soul doesn't know how to just be. Still.

On the merrier side, no matter the year or circumstance, Christmas joy can be like having an empty house to fill. We have the freedom to start from scratch. Because our faith is a fluid work and process, we can experience renewed hope and purpose in every season. Metaphorically speaking, there's no need to pick out the same pieces of furniture from Christmases past.

We don't have to choose the same busy pace, either. The hectic habits. The push and pressure. These forms of Christmas coping may have worked in the past, but now, maybe these mechanisms are lumpy and pilly and completely worn out.

Perhaps we can make it a point to be satisfied with less. Instead of a Christmas catch-all, we "miss out." We let the elf get dusty. The holidays have never been about what activities or traditions or events we plan or attend. Always, the holidays are about how much extra space we leave for the simplicity of the Savior's celebration to saturate our hearts. Our hearts are revived when we adopt a seasonal pace we can keep up with.

Finding Joy

It's super difficult to find the balance between simplicity and enthusiasm for the season, though. The sweet spot is somewhere between merry and what matters most. If we don't make some adjustments, even though the chaos may have slowed, our internal pressure can continue to drive us toward keeping up, keeping busy, and moving. Maybe even to the ... *gulp* ... laundry room.

It's great to take inventory of what we believe and feel to be most important about this time of year, and ask ourselves, *How do I want to celebrate the season?*

"And the angel said to them, "Fear not, for behold, I bring you good tidings of great joy that will be for all the people. "For unto you is born this day in the city of David, a Savior, who is Christ the Lord.'" (Luke 2:10-11). The angel's proclamation answers the question of how we may strive to celebrate...with great joy.

Great joy. That *will be* for all. That will continue. That doesn't change. This truth reminds us that joy is fixed and permanent. Ever present—not small. This same elation still waits to be found. And for me, someone who feels they might be missing out—the permanence of this promise is a relief. The joy I can have with Jesus? It isn't going anywhere.

Misplaced Hope

Sadly, there were so many souls who missed this One amazing, transforming, star-shining-bright-over-the-spot event in Bethlehem. We see this, "And all went to be registered, each to his own town" (Luke 2:1-3). So actually, many people showed up. The "all" used in this verse from Luke comes with the categorical context that *all* were there, but few were seeking Jesus. Jesus waited for them then like He waits for us now.

The thought that Jesus waits for me like this is life changing. I picture Him watching for His joy to be evident in the way I experience a day, or in how I pursue the gifts that He gives. And therefore, watching me miss out on stress and pressure and excess. Some days, though, I find myself busy looking ahead, sometimes missing the abundance which shines above. My pursuit of happiness quickly leads me away from wholeness, and I'm humbled to consider all I can misplace.

Finding Christmas

There is hope for the holidays. Because the happiness and truth of who Jesus is can't be taken away. In fact, we gain. "Furthermore, because we are united with Christs, we have received an inheritance from God, for he chose us in advance, and he makes everything work out according to his plan" (Ephesians 1:11 NLT).

As we seek Jesus at Christmas, we are eclipsed by worries and concerns. We may even forget that we left the elf and busyness behind. Because an inheritance of joy, peace, and goodness waits for us.

In place of all the festivities this Christmas, we can first consider what we don't want to miss. We have the freedom to start from scratch. To have the joy and peace that waits for us. Even to visit the laundry room if we want to. But who really wants to (other than the elf, that is)?

*Father, it's in You we have peace today. When we look for it
in other ways, coax us into your better house. Don't let us live
with a lot of cluttered worry or uncertain care. Keep us sifting.*

Sorting. May we clear room for Your simplicity—we make
everything so complicated, Lord. Your Word promises peace
as we draw close to You. And where You are is calm. Fill our
moments, our hours, our calendars with more of You. Always.
Amen.

The Thrill of Hope from Rhonda

Snow angels in powdered sugar? Yes, please. Let's add some chocolate and make it a real dessert, shall we? Still striving here, however, to add less (except for chocolate) to the calendar. Add less, pray more. More of the prayer Beth prayed so sweetly. Prayers of finding peace in the Father, moment by moment. Prayers of clearing out the worry-clutter and filling up instead on His promises, drawing closer to Him. We will ever find our sweet spot right there. With or without the powdered sugar.

Chapter 9

Up in My Brain There Arose Such a Clatter

Rhonda

"So prepare your minds for action, be completely sober [in spirit—steadfast, self-disciplined, spiritually and morally alert], fix your hope completely on the grace [of God] that is coming to you when Jesus Christ is revealed. [Live] as obedient children [of God]; do not be conformed to the evil desires which governed you in your ignorance [before you knew the requirements and transforming power of the good news regarding salvation]. But like the Holy One who called you, be holy yourselves in all your conduct [be set apart from the world by your godly character and moral courage]; because it is written, 'YOU SHALL BE HOLY (set apart), FOR I AM HOLY'" (1 Peter 1:13-16 AMP).

'm not sure I'm ever quite as strongly opinionated about anything in the world as I am when I'm tasked with the hanging of the evergreen garland on the front porch. I become a strange mix of overthinking and under-thinking and under-over-do-it-yourself-ing.

Small schwoops on that greenery? No, thanks—and don't be ridiculous. I'll allow no discussion on this. But not too big either. Keep in mind those schwoops must have some serious uniformity as well. I over/under-think it all. Placing and spacing, depth and breadth, length and strength (I don't actually have a strong opinion about the strength of the placement, I just really wanted the rhyme there).

When it's time to hang that Christmas greenery, please understand I'm going to need a tape measure and a yardstick. Yes, both. Maybe also a protractor and a compass. A quadrant and an astrolabe are not out of the question. Again, the funny thing is, I'll make a big to-do about the measurements, then about half an hour in, I'll start eyeballing it. But I'll probably be rather opinionated about that, too.

All that rigamarole is for the front porch greenery. Don't even get me started on the banister and the fireplace inside the house. I have three glue guns and a slew of bungee cords with hooks, and I know how to use them. Sort of. Either way, this stuff will be hung by the chimney. Maybe not always with care, but certainly with flair. And definitely with strong opinions.

Opinions—Oh, How I Have Them

So many opinions. On so many topics. All mine. Loud ones and high ones. Colorful and wry ones. I try to make sure I come up with three or four good opinions to have on standby, just in case somebody asks for one.

I'm not at all talking about "informed" opinions, mind you. Those are in an entirely different category. Informed opinions require research and contemplation. Reason and thinky stuff. Probably charts and graphs beyond my astrolabing. That sounds like work. Plus, if you get too informed on a topic, seems to me you no longer have an opinion. What you have there is a conclusion. Wouldn't that cancel out the need for an opinion?

A friend asked my opinion about Instagram several months

ago. I told her I was great at Instagram opinions and that I figure I'm only about one extra-large floppy hat away from becoming an Insta spokesmodel. She said that was a delusion, not an opinion.

Delusions, Illusions, and Better Conclusions

Still, I recently heard someone offer an opinion that was even worse than any of mine. We all hear this one a lot. "Go with your gut."

What? My *gut*? Like I'm not getting rotten enough ideas from my brain, now we're going to check in with my colon? How is that better?

How about this for something better. Instead of forming baseless opinions and going with our innards, what if we prepared our minds the Jesus way, set our hope firmly on His grace, and made decisions based on the rightness and holiness of God?

Like this: "Therefore, preparing your minds for action, and being sober-minded, set your hope fully on the grace that will be brought to you at the revelation of Jesus Christ. As obedient children, do not be conformed to the passions of your former ignorance, but as he who called you is holy, you also be holy in all your conduct" (1 Peter 1:13-15).

Gut Checks and Mind Preps

To prepare your minds for action in the original context was to gather up the constraining robes so that a person could move forward unhindered. Hindrances begin in our minds as we let thoughts and opinions run rambly-like from brain to gut and back, unfettered. Such a clatter in the gray matter.

Our actions are birthed in our minds. We're called to be diligent—actively self-controlled—about what goes on in our headspace. In the Christmas season. In every season. Not necessarily ready with some wild opinion you can hang your greenery on. But ever ready to replace self-thinking and worldly philosophies with the truth of God. Ready as well to let that thinking birth obedience and right living and fulfill a holy calling from a holy God to a life of holiness.

Conforming to the passions of our former ignorance, that unregenerate way of forming opinions, produces a continuous and frustrating inner battle. It's so much worse than eyeballing it. The ready mind Peter encourages is not one that excuses or rationalizes sinful thoughts. The ready mind reins them in—rolling up the sleeves of our thoughts and putting them to work for the Kingdom, all in the power of Christ.

This Is Not a Solo Mission

It's fruitless to try to fight the mind battle on our own. Paul reminds us, "For the weapons of our warfare are not of the flesh but have divine power to destroy strongholds. We destroy arguments and every lofty opinion raised against the knowledge of God, and take every thought captive to obey Christ" (2 Corinthians 10:4-5 CSB).

Fleshly weapons are not weapons at all. Trying to enter into spiritual warfare with our own thinking, reasoning, and lofty opinions would be like taking on a DIY project with a glue gun and no glue. Put down that glue gun.

Yet we see victory as we enter the battle with any thought that's contrary to God's truth in opinion jail. The knowledge of God will lead us to victorious living.

So much for every "lofty opinion" because, yes, there is blessing, fruit, and a mind at peace as our thoughts are Jesus-captivated. This, I'm not afraid to say, is an informed opinion. Informed by the truth of who the Christ of Christmas is—and how powerfully He works in us.

I'm sticking firmly with that opinion. No glue gun needed. And I'm not even once checking to see what my intestines might think.

Lord, replace any worldly philosophies that may be rambling around in my brain with Your perfect truth. Ready me for right thinking that leads to obedience. Lead me in a holy walk, following You, my holy God. Make me starkly aware of any time I pick up a fleshly weapon to fight a spiritual battle. Lord, I want to leave every battle to You. Please use me in whatever way You will to destroy strongholds and accomplish Your will.

Merry and Bright from Beth

If I could fix things by thinking way too much about them—I totally would. Being an over-thinker fix-her-upper is a thing, *I think*. But Paul addresses this need to think about Jesus over and above and more often than anything else when he spoke of what Jesus' life accomplished: "Christ died for our sins, just as Scripture said" (1 Corinthians 15:3). Not only are we to think about Jesus, but to pass on what we know. The birth of Jesus was God's great hand come down to save us. Glorious to think about. Even more transforming to talk about.

Chapter 10

Fix Her Supper

Beth

*"They broke bread in their homes and ate together with glad
and sincere hearts" (Acts 2:46 NIV).*

These days have been a little different. Right? Wave your hands wildly if you've cut your own bangs, cut the dog's bangs, and cooked 1,032 meals for your family in the past many months. Plus, what about the holidays says "cooking"? Everything, I think. So, to help save time with all the meal preparation, I … planted an herb garden the size of a football field.

It's rare for me to get excited about something so tiny, but did you know God created a delicious-looking herb called Boxwood Basil? It's the tiniest edible tree. For Christmas' sake, I may bring it in and string twinkle lights on it. But Christmas aside, it's seriously too cute to cook with. Or eat.

My husband, however, wants to know what it tastes like. Funny guy. I had to explain to him that you don't really *eat it*. You just look at it. Smell it. Pat it on its leafy little head and let it give you life. Cut its bangs sometimes.

I may not cook with boxwood basil, but I do love to prepare food for family and friends. I love to serve them and make a fuss over their lives. Over their day. Over their ... turkey?

Yes, the past few Thanksgivings I've discovered how to brine a turkey. If you've never prepped poultry this way, you may be missing out. *May be?* At least this turkey prep forces me to defrost the turkey earlier than my typical frozen, panicked night before.

No Harm. No Fowl?

Last Thanksgiving, despite my "early bird" planning, I was still in the rear in preparation. I'm still not quite sure how I prepared ahead to be so far behind. The late night before Thanksgiving, I hurled ice and broth and all the herbs in the house (except boxwood basil), into a container and shut the lid. I knew the turkey knew what to do.

Only I didn't.

Then on Thanksgiving Day, the oven buzzed, and I placed the steamy main course on the top of the stove. I stared at it. The red popper? Popped. The skin? Crisp-eee. The meat ... *uh...* I broke the news first to my brother-in-law who had the gravy baster in hand and ready. "So, something is wrong with this turkey, Greg. Where did all the meat go?"

I could only guess that the make-haste-pace upset the fussy fowl. And I'm not dramatizing here. The bulk of the turkey looked like it had evaporated. You know the sound of champagne glasses clinking and cheers ringing? Or the *Woot-Woot* from hungry-turkey-people as they watch you carve? Well, that was happening at *your* house. Not mine.

I told Greg that the gravy boat was going nowhere and laughed until a few tired tears leaked out.

Then it dawned on me. Smacked me like a stuck electric knife, literally. Because I realized I was trying to slice into the gluteus maximus of the turkey and not the other side. I mean, I knew I was "behind" in the prep, but ... well ... I had cooked the turkey upside-down! Obviously, opposite of what I wanted to do. Sharp contrasts can ignite lasting impressions though.

How to Set the Holiday Table

Just like being apart these past months can make us appreciate "together" even more, even when life turns upside down, our reason to enjoy each other doesn't diminish. It's as bright as ever, and "in your light do we see light" (Psalm 36:9). When we take time to know Jesus, we see just how relational He is.

Scripture helps us see the love Jesus has as He sits on a vast mountainside. Then as He gathers at the long and lengthy gathering table. His hospitality reminds us to make room for more.

One of the greatest commandments: "Love your neighbor as yourself" (Mark 12:31), tells us how important loving others is to loving God.

And what better way to love than to spend time at the gathering table? When we look at the Greek word for "together," it's translated as *homos*: To be at the same place or time together. God knows a sense of belonging and closeness is central to our hearts. But how often are we in the same room, same vicinity, or same atmosphere doing so many different things? Apart.

Togetherness is what Jesus modeled as He nourished those around Him. Like the invite to the chief tax collector. Jesus told Zacchaeus to come down from the tree. "Zacchaeus, hurry and come down, for I must stay at your house today" (Luke 19:5). We can learn from the way Christ pursued others. When I studied this story, I also noticed this, "And he was seeking to see who Jesus was ..." (vs. 3). Zacchaeus wanted to see Jesus. Not just look at Him, he wanted to know more about the core of who Jesus was. It was like Zacchaeus was the living example of how to pursue fellowship with one another—and with Christ—reminding us to, "Oh, taste and see that the Lord is good!" (Psalm 34:8).

Jesus Didn't Come to Fix Stuff

I have never chewed on an idea so much: a modest dinner invite becomes an opportunity for someone to see Jesus. And a chance to demonstrate to others who Jesus is (maybe for the first time). Could fellowship be any more delicious?

We need each other. We can discover intimacy with communion and gain insight through fellowship. More importantly, closeness communicates there's room enough to belong, and spending time together at the gathering table leads to moments of sincere connection.

I guess it's no shocker that I too often forgo connection while every little strain gobbles me up. Sometimes, I secretly want God to fix all the mess and problems and set the metaphoric table for me.

Scripture tells us many people wanted the same thing from God when He walked this earth. As Jesus accepts an invitation for dinner from Simon in Luke chapter 7, the Pharisee has reason to believe Jesus will discuss and solve hot topics like Jewish law, leadership, and religious rules of the day. But then we see this, "…and he went into the Pharisee's house and reclined at the table" (v. 36).

Here, Jesus shows us that being together offers us a valuable gift—time to gather, slow down, and connect in soul-deep ways. And is it just me, or does this gesture from Jesus to "recline" make Him even more relatable? It appears Jesus didn't just show up on earth to fix stuff. He came for intimate, and forever-lasting togetherness.

During this same dinner at Simon's house, an additional uninvited woman enters, and it says she "came with a bottle of very expensive perfume and stood at his feet, weeping, raining tears on his feet" (Luke 7:37 The Message). Sweet tears. Sweet joy. Sweet Jesus. Our Savior savors beautiful people interruptions, doesn't He?

And here's the amazing thing. Jesus didn't come to set things right side up—although He totally did—but to nurture as we do this life upside down.

We can do the holidays differently than the crazy rate you might expect. We can love others differently than they expect while we gather.

I'm reminded this year to make Christmas less about touchy turkeys and to-dos and various topsy-turvies. More about just being together. You could say that not taking the time to enjoy each other is like patting a boxwood basil on the head instead of tasting it. Can you imagine? Errr … ok. Let me clarify. This is only a hypothetical example for imagining, as opposed to actually … gulp … *eating* the adorabasil. No. We would never.

> *Jesus, You came to nourish us. You brought bread for the hungry, love for the unloved, hope for those who were spiritually deprived. Your birth brought healing for a hurting world. It feeds us with the harvest of abundant life. Your love is delicious in every way. Love brought You down; love brings us together to celebrate it. May we set the table for more this Christmas; grow our thirst and magnify our hunger for You.*

The Thrill of Hope with Rhonda

So true, these past upside-down months have inspired us to love and appreciate our "together" so much more. May we celebrate our Savior well and revel in the love He has shown us. And may we be receptive and even excited about the way He empowers us to extend that delicious love to others as well.

Meanwhile, Beth is right, I'm so over the cooking thing. I've been at least a little over it since before I ever started it. So reader-friend, what time should I arrive for dinner?

Chapter 11

Flights of Not-So-Fancy

Rhonda

"Therefore, my beloved brothers and sisters, be steadfast,
immovable, always excelling in the work of the Lord
[always doing your best and doing more than is needed],
being continually aware that your labor [even to the point of
exhaustion] in the Lord is not futile nor wasted [it is never
without purpose]"
(1 Corinthians 15:58 AMP).

I was trying to come up with a great Christmas themed Fix Her Upper kind of joke. One that would really sleigh you. *Sleigh* you? Get it?

Sorry, but we still might make that work. What if we talked about a certain decorative vintage sleigh that's at least one reindeer short of a full team? Nah. I should probably try to *rein* in the reindeer-related quips. It be-*hooves* me to move on.

Yes, moving on. Though not necessarily up. Because when it

comes time to put that DIYed sleigh on the roof, forgive me, but I'll be the one keeping both feet on the ground. I might steady the ladder for you. But I don't do roofs. It's not that I'm afraid of falling off the roof, you understand. I'm not afraid of the falling. I'm afraid of the landing. It's the thought of the splat at the end that keeps me off that ladder altogether.

And Other Tall Tales

It's a similar story with sleigh-flying or skydiving—except taller still. There are several reasons I'll never skydive, for instance. I'll give you my top two. First, I've seen videos of people skydiving. Their faces … well … they "flutter." Wildly. Honestly, I don't need to see my face flapping violently over my ears, thank you very much. That kind of wind velocity is just not meant for faces over 40. It ends up looking like a basset hound pup with its head out a car window—multiplied by however many years you are over 40.

I'm not daring enough to sass the math. Gravity plus wind velocity times the number of years over 40. That's an equation that can't equal anything pretty.

But in addition to the math of it all, the second reason you won't find me sleigh-flying or skydiving—and the biggest reason—is this simple: gravity. Higher reasoning than even my thoughts on lights and ladders. Seems to me skydiving could all too easily become sky-*dying*. Again, it's not even the jumping out of a plane part that scares me so much as it is the inevitability of the hitting the ground part. It's true, it's not really the jumping, or even the falling. It's the landing. And the continued possibility of it ending in a splat. Sometimes I wonder if people who skydive don't really understand the *gravity* of the situation.

Gotta Stick That Landing

That reminds me, though, how glad I am that I know where I'm headed, eternally speaking. I don't fear death. I will confess here, I do fear pain. Actually it's not quite fear of pain. It's more of a very vigorously enthusiastic hatred of pain. A vigorously enthusiastic whine-filled hatred.

But pain or no pain, it's essential we know that because of the

Christ of Christmas, our future is secure and that death, however it comes, is not the end. There's amazing comfort there. And that always puts fear in its place. It even puts math in its place.

2 Corinthians 4:1: "Therefore, having this ministry by the mercy of God, we do not lose heart."

A few verses later in 2 Corinthians 4:16-18, Paul picks it up again. "So we do not lose heart. Though our outer self is wasting away, our inner self is being renewed day by day. For this light momentary affliction is preparing for us an eternal weight of glory beyond all comparison, as we look not to the things that are seen but to the things that are unseen. For the things that are seen are transient, but the things that are unseen are eternal."

The Amplified version of verse 17 refers to our existence on the other side of this flappy-faced life as "an everlasting weight of glory, beyond all measure, excessively surpassing all comparisons and all calculations, a vast and transcendent glory and blessedness never to cease!" Now that, my friends, is a weight that defies gravity. This is some math I can love. It's a beyond-all-measure, never-ceasing glory. Its calculations are beyond comparison in this life. No need to bother with any old equation. This is the greatest of the "greater thans."

For the Then and for the Now

The "vast and transcendent glory and blessedness never to cease"—what an exciting description of our eternity. But the unseen "eternal things" are not reserved exclusively for heaven. These are truths that make a vital difference in our everyday. Knowing our future impacts our present. It emboldens us, strengthens us, helps us "not lose heart" in the here and now.

David said in Psalm 27:14, "Wait for the Lord; be strong and take heart and wait for the Lord" (NIV). Lose heart? Nope. Take it! We take heart as we wait for, hope in, and trust completely our Lord God. David reminds us often that we need not fear falling, spiritually speaking—no matter how tall the ladder. "Be strong and take heart, all you who hope in the Lord" (Psalm 31:24 NIV). There it is again. *Take* heart!

Jesus Himself gives us the best reason to take heart in John

16:33. "I have said these things to you, that in me you may have peace. In the world you will have tribulation. But take heart; I have overcome the world."

Follow in Taking, Follow in Not Losing

I want to follow Jesus, my Savior who has overcome all, and "take heart." I want to follow Paul's instructions well and "not lose heart." Instead of losing my heart, I want to make extra sure I take heart, and then keep it. I know it's some strange math, but I think keeping my heart means giving it away. A heart fully surrendered to Christ is one that is able to look past the pains and problems of this life— and to look past a wildly flapping, wasting-away face—and experience renewal day by day. That's the best way to fix-her-up a Christmas. O that we may live in that renewal, living this life well in the power of the One who created us. I want that. And then, I want to finish well. I want to stick the landing, and that's that. With or without the splat.

Father, thank You for redeeming my heart. Keep it, I ask. Let my trust in You make me steadfast, immovable, always excelling in Your work, always doing my best and doing more than is needed, and continually aware that even the most exhausting labor is never wasted or without purpose (1 Corinthians 15:15 AMP). Let me take heart and never lose heart. Be my purpose, my strength, the heart of my heart. May I finish well, in and through Jesus.

Merry and Bright from Beth

I wouldn't mind skydiving if I could fall gently. And not so fast. Once, my dog took me for a brisk walk and launched me into the air. Surprisingly, you don't really stick when you land that hard— you bounce. You break your shoulder. BAM! Even that tiny accident built new things in me. A new perspective and healing. And new and creative ways to put on makeup. It's true that our life isn't more secure because it remains unchanged, unbroken or grounded (well, grounded is good). But each day we can move in God's direction. His way is always toward peace, hope, and lofty love.

Chapter 12

Reframing Christmas

Beth

*"And the Word was made flesh, and dwelt among us, (and we
beheld his glory, the glory as of the only begotten of the Father,)
full of grace and truth" (John 1:14 KJV).*

I was shopping the other day with my daughter when she asked,
"Do you think this jumpsuit looks like it will fit ok?" Yes, it looked
adorable on the hanger with stripes and baggy legs and a ONE SIZE
FITS ALL label. So, not being permitted to try it on didn't matter for
her, nor for anyone. Apparently. Besides, on the hanger the jumper
looked like it was totally going to work.

Except. It. Didn't. Bless her 5'10" long frame.

Back at home, she laughed as she stepped into the kitchen to
model her new jumper for us. And that's when we realized, she'd tried
on a tightly fitted, short ... sock? She looked like the sweetest stocking

stuffer. The boho look she was going for? Well, that ideal was done. I can say this with certainty. Why? Because I tried on the same outfit with the thought it could fit my shorter frame.

But I was wrong.

I can say with all certainty that ONE SIZE DOES NOT FIT ALL! At least, that's what I figured out when I couldn't get the outfit to come off. Brooklyn had to help me. Then we laugh-cried so hard about it, maybe things should totally not fit more often.

The thought of one outfit fitting everyone in the universe is really the best kind of optimism. Especially at Christmas. But there is a huge chasm between the real deal and the looks-so-cute-on-the-hanger-ideal. *Come on, jumper label people. No one wants to wear a body-sock for Christmas.* It's true, things don't always fit.

Measure Once, Cut Three Times

It's easy to try to stuff big ideas into a smaller reality. Take a Christmas tree, for example. Out in the giant world and field, a stately conifer appears as if it's going to work, and it is a "Honey, that tree will fit," debate every time.

Once you drag the tree from the field to the truck though, the tree has time to grow. That's the only explanation for the mismeasurement. Because then your husband has to cut 3 feet off the trunk while you realize that your eyes may have been bigger than your Toyota. That's when you propose to build on to the house and make the tree work. And there is the slightest chance my husband now carries a measuring tape to all the Christmas tree farms we frequent.

There was one time when the tree really was too big. Some family members may have had to squeeze chairs outside the sunroom, into the kitchen. And the tree sap is still sticking to our walls. We may have our measuring issues at the Duewel house, but we could agree that ridiculousness stood 12 foot and too many inches high.

It's true, Christmas can hold a bit of dread for me, though. You know, with all the extra stocking stuffers and hoopla I hang on the mantel. But I've learned that we don't have to hammer unnecessary holes into the way we feel about this occasion. Or get weary trying to hit the mark, *Is this enough, or a little too much? Are all the hopes I have for the holiday gonna fit?*

A One Size Really Does Fit All

Whether it's sitting quietly in reflection of Christmas or being the faithful first to the tree farm. These joys are all a special part of the season for us. Christ is the one who makes it personal and precious. We can toss all the guilt into the winter wind. Thank goodness, Jesus' love doesn't need tried-on or measured out. He offers a truly one size fits all invitation.

This is important to remember. Especially this Christmas. For Pete's sake, I hung a banner in my kitchen that reads HAPPY BIRTHADY. Too funny. The sign came this way. I can't fix it, nor do I even want to. And because this is the day we are living in, I may want to reframe it right along with my thinking. There is new hope as we accept today's oddities but live Christmas with clarity.

Besides, focusing on the true gift of Jesus' birth always puts me in the right frame of mind. Christ's love steadfast, we don't have to worry if we're doing Christmas right. Clearly Jesus already did.

His rightness starts with this reminder: "The Word became flesh and dwelt among us" (John 1:14). Here Jesus tells us who God is. And let's reread the verse, honestly, because it just doesn't always sink in how well God loves us. The first chapter of John tells us that Jesus is completely, fully, and wholly God. God's expression of love lived out in human form.

In this verse from John, Jesus is described as the "Word." The Greek reference for Word here is *Logos,* which means to be identical to God and co-creator with God. How much more personal can God get than to come down from perfection and live?

And try this on for size; Christmas is the mark and moment God became personal to us. His love? Tailored to fit.

Holy Comes to the Unholy Fit

How does this relate to us?

We can study God's Word and pray and go to church, but if

we don't believe the promise of Christmas and the gift Jesus gave freely, well, we may worry God could change His mind about us. Worse yet, that His love changes according to our behavior or our struggles with sin. Or that we will never measure up to His devotion. But that's the point, we don't have to. Jesus met every requirement. You want immeasurable hope?

Let's revel in the enormity of grace as we read this. "For unto us a Child is born, unto us a Son is given" (Isaiah 9:6 KJV). This verse? With its "to us" reference is the truth of how underserved and universal and gracious the gift was that God wrapped for us … *unto us a child was born.*

Having children has taught me with a renewed clarity that any present offered with the principle of deserving is hardly a present at all. Nothing in me has ever earned pure attention from God. Nothing. Yet, "for unto us" tells us we're worth the gift we've been offered. Before Jesus, we were unacceptable to a Holy God, and wholly unable to repair ourselves. Let's try this on for size: "For a child has been born—for us! The gift of a son—for us! He'll take over the running of the world. His names will be: Amazing Counselor, Strong God, Eternal Father, Prince of Wholeness. His ruling authority will grow, and there'll be no limits to the wholeness he brings" (Isaiah 9:6-7 The Message).

The staggering question in all this: Why did God try to fit into our world, when we are so unfit to grace the doorway of His? But Isaiah offers us immeasurable hope, boundless joy, and limitless love. God's love does not fit—but here it is.

Now that I think about it, things should totally *not* fit more often.

Jesus, we can try to build our lives as we see fit. It never works. My faith, a work in progress. Help me live every minute of every day finding the truth in Your firm foundation. If You were to measure me, Lord, if You were to write the length of my lack, my life would come up infinity short. Forever lost to sin. But Your sacrifice filled in the space of my separation from You. Thank You. My effort is never enough to make up the difference of Your holy. Yet You came down. Lately, I seldom know why

*certain things are happening. Or why a circumstance doesn't
work or flow. But we can trust You even when life doesn't seem
to measure up. Your ways are Sovereign. Your plan mighty.
Rebuild our faith this Christmas while You show us the right
way to love. Help us remember how perfectly Your love came
down, and how wonderfully it frames our hope. Amen.*

Thrill of Hope from Rhonda

I'm so thankful God made a salvation plan for us that just fits. No wait, it's a salvation plan that's even bigger than we need. There's room to spare and grace for every bulge. I love Beth's reminder that in the mind and heart of our Father, we were worth the gift of His Son. What an astounding, humbling, heart-altering, hope-restoring, life-giving gift. In the midst of all the gift-giving this season, let's focus on the greatest Gift, the Gift of all gifts: Jesus. Oh how we celebrate the gift of His birth.

And only you friends will get it when I say with the merriest, most thankful heart: HAPPY BIRTHADY, Jesus!

Chapter 13

Seasoning the Season

Rhonda

*"I will remember the deeds of the LORD; yes, I will remember
your wonders of old. I will ponder all your work, and meditate
on your mighty deeds. Your way, O God, is holy. What god is
great like our God?" (Psalm 77:11-13).*

Here it is. The most useful idea for a pre-holiday construction project. A vigorous reinforcement of the dining table.

I wish I could remember to set this project in motion at a more appropriate time of the year, but I seem to forget until the Christmas season is here. Then it gets real. Because we're unquestionably going to need sturdier dining tables, friends. I'm talking about the kind of dining table that can hold up uncompromisingly under the average American Christmas party buffet. Truss that thing. Bolster, brace, and bracket it. Better use steel. There's no place in this time of year for a wobbly table. No one wants to be a large party tray or two away from a catastrophic table failure and a heartbreaking, disastrous finger food breach. A canape-covered floor? That's just too sad. For everyone except maybe the dog.

Incidentally, the only thing more impressive than how much we can load onto a buffet table is how much I can load onto one plate. It's one plate, and it's all only for me. Still mounds and mounds. I don't know why I feel I can't be the person who goes back to the table again. But I do know that I'm compelled to load four trips' worth of sticky chicken wings onto that one paper plate. A plate which also needs some serious reinforcement. Plate on plate on plate.

Other Christmas Greenery

Before I'm forced to start triple stack plating, I should try to remember some important dietary principles and ask myself a question or two. Like, "would it hurt you to throw a salad in there every now and then?"

It's interesting that I've discovered something rather disturbing about myself on that topic: I'm a salad dressing whiny-baby. It's not like I'm even all that into salad. I think we all know I'd rather have chocolate. Or coffee. Or chocolate mixed with coffee. But the other day I found myself with a salad that needed something that neither coffee nor chocolate could fix (though it took me several minutes to come to grips with that). So there I stood at a restaurant salad bar (suitably reinforced, by the way) trying all the salad dressings. All of them. I even mixed a few—like some sort of mad scientist. The first dressing was too tart. The next one, too sweet. Then the next one was just too ... orange.

That's when I figured out that I was not so much a mad scientist. No. I was Goldilocks.

Don't Spoil the Dressing

When did I become so dressing-spoiled? It doesn't even comfort me all that much that I'm not the only one. God's chosen people had wandered in the desert for 40 years because they had chosen not to trust the Lord. When they finally stood poised to enter the land of promise, instead of the "now you can all relax" message they might've expected, they got more of a "don't get too spoiled" warning.

"Be careful that you don't forget the Lord your God by failing to keep His command … When you eat and are full, and build beautiful houses to live in, and your herds and flocks grow large, and your silver and gold multiply, and everything else you have increases, be careful that your heart doesn't become proud and you forget the Lord your God …" (Deuteronomy 8:11-14 HCSB).

In the verses just prior to these, the people are reminded to be diligent in their obedience to God because "the Lord your God is bringing you into a good land … a land of wheat, barley, vines, figs, and pomegranates; a land of olive oil and honey," (Deuteronomy 8:7-8). Olive oil and honey? They were headed into the best salads with all the best dressings.

A Christmas to Remember

The entire chapter of Deuteronomy 8 is full of "remembers" and "don't forgets." And it's not just the Israelites. It's so often in our times of greatest blessing even now that we forget our Lord God is the source of that blessing and that "every perfect gift is from above, coming down from the Father of lights," (James 1:17 HCSB). Anytime we forget, the blessing loses its sweetness. Pride replaces recognition of His provision and our satisfaction in life sours.

Can a season get sort of "over-seasoned"? I think we truly can overload it like an overdone Christmas buffet table. How ironic that as we're deep into the celebration of the birth of our Savior, we can get overloaded with the activities of it all and forget the glorious inspiration of those activities and the object of our worship. Worshiping an activity is empty. Bowing to a celebration is meaningless. Going through the motions of Christmas without remembering why Jesus came and what He accomplished for us through His coming is ignoring everything that's "just right" about the celebration. A Christmas to remember happens as we truly remember. Him.

When we catch ourselves going all Goldilocks-y in all the wrong ways, it should trigger our reminder to … well … "remember." "You may say to yourself, 'My power and my own ability have gained this wealth for me,' but remember that the Lord your God gives you the power to gain wealth," (Deuteronomy 8:17-18 HCSB).

You Must Remember This

The right remembering throughout the season of celebration—and all year long—can reinforce our faith and allow Christmas to become a season of growth. Who doesn't want a faith that will hold up as uncompromisingly as a steel-reinforced buffet table? No catastrophic fail, thanks.

The passage in Deuteronomy 8 gives us a check. Remembering that every good blessing is from Him helps keep our obnoxious pride in check and reminds us to lean on Him for everything, big and small. It reminds us to love, follow, trust, and obey. And that adds blessing upon blessing—whatever we do, wherever we go—whatever is on the menu.

Meanwhile, I hope you'll excuse me. I have once again over-buffet-ed myself and salad is on the menu for a few days. Think I'll try making my own dressing. So now it appears I must travel to a thousand islands.

Father, I intentionally remember You in this very moment. You are my great and gracious Provider. I have nothing good that You have not given me. You are mighty. You are good. You are giving. You are loving. You are my God who saves. Help me to remember the miraculous salvation plan that was set into motion as Your Son, Jesus, was born into this world. Reinforce my remembering, I ask. I never, ever want to forget. May my blessings inspire thanks and praise and more remembering, never forgetfulness. I pray You will help me get rid of any meaningless activity I've mindlessly loaded onto the schedule. Replace it, I pray, with conscious, deliberate remembering and sincere worship. I. Remember. You.

Merry and Bright from Beth

We are working on a bathroom reno and hope to be done by Christmas. But it's taken longer than we thought, and now I can't remember the pre-reno plans we made before the post-reno mess. A blueprint would've been a good plan. That's why I love this bit from Hebrews 8, "For the Lord your God is bringing you into a good land..." (v. 7). When we're stuck in a mess, it's great to remember the good place God is going. I want to remember that Christmas is God's best plan. Now, if I could just remember what color I chose for the bathroom walls.

Chapter 14

What Happened Was We Had a Little Trouble with the Tree

Beth

"They entered the house and saw the child with his mother, Mary, and they bowed down and worshiped him. Then they opened their treasure chests and gave him gifts of gold, frankincense, and myrrh" (Matthew 2:11 NLT)

I am a big fan of tree farms. Every year our family's Christmas cheer kicks off as we cut through the snow with leathery boots to find just the right tree. I'll admit, I can pack a ridiculous amount of effort into this tradition. I have no restraint.

While my husband is willing to twirl a few evergreens for inspection, he cannot abide by my typical undecided four or five. I've learned this. Usually, what happens is, I can't make a decision, and the conifer which reaches the highest and loses the fewest number of needles after my non-stop fussing with it, wins.

One Christmas though, there was this thing.

After chasing Christmas trees—we'd found *the* tree. Then, we hauled it inside our home only to realize it had a whole condominium full of left-behind "furniture" from squirrels (maybe even racoons) within its branches. Even Jerry, who is pretty patient and rational with things like this, wanted to know, "How in the world did we *not* see this mess?" Completely frustrated, we trudged the tree back outside to demo the disaster.

When we finally placed the newly-detailed pine back into the stand that night, though, when we admired it and turned it 52 more times to find just the right angle, we discovered … there *was* no right angle. And what I want to tell you is that the trunk of the evergreen was flawed and crooked and never going to stand straight, no matter how many times we spun it around. The shorter story: We heaved the tree off the back porch. It took a time-out.

Chasing Christmas

Can I just explain here how many powerful and contradictory emotions surface at Christmastime? Quite possibly you've noticed them too. The big feelings, sometimes even bigger expectations, converge into a big ol' deal. And then your Christmas tree lays in your backyard for a whole week. In the snow. With a little tinsel stuck to it.

Back to the tree—avoidable no longer—Jerry and I finally tethered it to the corner of our living room and called it done. Ho-ho-hum.

This crazy, chasing-Christmas-tree me is not the better me. It's a mystery why we chose to let an easy trial like a crooked tree trunk crack our emotional stamina like that. It could have been the stress we were under that day. The struggle we were in. Or the expectation of the season that we succumbed to. Just so many merry messes can factor in here.

I have come to savor this memory of Christmas-tree-gone-wrong more than any other Christmas disaster (because we've had a few). Because when my expectations are taken down to the ~~ground~~

snow like that, it's easier to remember how desperately I need to pursue something more. I've learned being thrilled with the celebration of Christmas and being elated with my Savior are simply not the same thing.

But here is the hope. We can have both.

Embracing Expectations

We can have the happy time of fellowship and family and fun-filled gift giving. And enjoy the trek out to get the family tree. Sure, we're going to have some drifts in the snow, but despite the struggles we endure, where we see bad, God sees good. God takes an approach to Christmas we don't expect. Just look at 1 Corinthians 15:57. "But thanks be to God, who gives us the victory through our Lord Jesus Christ." We can expect victory because Jesus is victorious!

Jesus was born. Died. And rose from death to live forever. Because Jesus came and conquered sin and struggle, we have a belongingness to the Christmas story. Like, we are *in* it with Him as He wins it. Exactly why the Christmas season is a wonderful time of joy and celebration. Also, some valid expectations. But it's important that we don't allow tree chasing to overtake us and mess with how much we partake in this great season of joy. We may want to keep our striving straight. *clearing throat here*

By all means, feel free to throw any unreasonable hopes out into the snow and let them think about all they've done. Remembering: It's not the Christmas pace we're chasing, but the person who *is* Christmas that we're so eager to see.

We can be equally anxious and excited for new and fresh in any season of our lives. Maybe we don't just push through harder, we sigh softer. We consider that the thrill of hope is not in the making, doing, or choosing the "right one." Then comes the relief: Anytime we fix our heart and hope on the source of the season—in celebration and great expectation—we honor Jesus.

Our Bold Hope

Another look at the book of Matthew, and we're reminded that it's a win-win for us. Every Christmastime.

"Behold, the virgin shall conceive and bear a son, and they shall call his name Immanuel (which means God with us)" (Matthew 1:23).

Here an angel of God has appeared to Joseph in a dream proclaiming the hope of Jesus' birth. The angel begins his declaration with the word behold. The word in Greek is *horao*, translated as a "pay attention to" and "don't miss this" exclamation. This is such an easy reminder for me to celebrate the season with an exclamation point. To pay attention that Jesus is the big deal and exclamation of Christmas.

Then we read the verse at the top of this chapter again, "And going into the house, they saw the child with Mary his mother, and they fell down and worshiped him. Then, opening their treasures, they offered him gifts, gold and frankincense and myrrh" (Matthew 2:11). The Magi's response can empower us. We don't know how many Magi looked for Jesus. Or how long they journeyed. Only that they looked. They found. They fell. They were so overwhelmed and excited to *behold* Jesus that they fell on their knees in bold exclamation of Jesus' birth. Reiterating that our eagerness for Christmas isn't the problem. Our enthusiasm with decorating? Not even an issue. And the giant deal with the trees? For me, kinda a given. But our hearts can *behold* a much greater hope!

Speaking of trees, my husband suggested we get an artificial one this year. But I'm still rooting for the real smell of pine in the house. Just don't be surprised if you drive by and see a tree lying out in the front yard. No worries. That's just me giving my expectations a much-needed timeout.

Authors note: Maybe you noticed a few football team references up and "down" these pages. I felt I needed to respond to my husband's joke about this chapter that, "I just thought there'd be more football in it." Ha! This chapter is a ho-ho-home run for me, sisters. *OH …* touchdown!

Jesus, You are the pursuit of my day and hope of all tomorrows.
We behold this Christmas and all the hope it brings close to our
hearts, but sometimes we lose sight of the truth of all we are
chasing. Keep us in the joy and anticipation of You, our eyes
looking and our hopes fixed on You.

Thrill of Hope with Rhonda

Did somebody order a thrill of hope? Okay, no matter what this section is titled, I know this kind of hope doesn't come from me. All hope is from Jesus. Jesus IS our hope. And I'm going to hang onto Beth's reminder that life is not about the chase and the pace. No, it's about the Person. The One we are so eager to see. All my hope is in Him.

On an unrelated note and an unrelated hope, I hope we all get Beth a bunch of pine-scented candles for Christmas this year. Surely that would be safer for everybody.

Chapter 15

No Wonder There's No Wonder

Rhonda

"For everyone born of God is victorious and overcomes the world; and this is the victory that has conquered and overcome the world—our [continuing, persistent] faith [in Jesus the Son of God]. Who is the one who is victorious and overcomes the world? It is the one who believes and recognizes the fact that Jesus is the Son of God" (1 John 5:4-5 AMP).

The lines are starting to blur. More accurately, my vision may be a little blurred on account of losing count of the number of lines. How many times have I stood in line (line after line after line) to check out at this one particular craft store? Better questions, how could I have taken on enough holiday projects to warrant 480 trips to this store, and how could I possibly have spent this much time in line here? Weeks and weeks of vision-blurring line-standing, right? I wonder how many sugarplum-ish-looking wreaths one person should make per season. Isn't there a limit? Because I feel like there should be a limit.

Sometimes I wonder if I'm spending my entire Christmas season in line. Ready. Set. WAIT.

People do say it's the season of wonder. So much wonder. I was in an express line at a department store the other day doing some intense wondering. First, I was wondering how they could label it "express." I'd been in that line for over half an hour, and that did not feel at all "express." But then maybe I'm not "expressing" myself well here [clearing throat].

Second, I was wondering why there was mistletoe hanging at every checkout. What, they want to give me a smooch to make me feel better about all the waiting? Don't take this the wrong way, but please don't do me any favors, cashier-people.

Mistletoe It and Make It Better?

Or hey, maybe the mistletoe is there so that after spending yet another half-hour waiting in line, we can kiss our Christmas cheer goodbye.

Visions of sugarplums? That's a big nope. Not even sugarless plums. No plums in the line at all. It's a plum-less line.

It's easy to get a little lost in all that plumless hustle and bustle of the season. How is it we can still feel all hustley/bustley even when we're standing reasonably still, waiting in line? We don't have to wonder why there's no wonder.

Wonder-empty vs. Wonder-full

Oh how disappointing it is when we're left wondering why the real wonder of Christmas has slipped away. The really real wonder. The sweetness. The blessed meaning. Christmas is not meant to over-stress or overwhelm us. It's not meant for overdoing or overspending. It's meant for celebrating how Jesus Christ, the Son of God, has come into this world so we could be made overcomers. First John 5:5 says, "Who is it that overcomes the world except the one who believes that Jesus is the Son of God?"

Jesus is the One who makes us overcomers as we believe, trust, and rest in Him. Isn't it amazing that as we truly rest in Him, we experience an amazing Christmas gift: peace! Jesus said, "I have said these things to you, that in me you may have *peace*. In the world you will have tribulation. But take heart; I have overcome the world" (John 16:33).

Jesus didn't mince words. He truly is the One who overcomes. And the One who makes us overcomers. And the One who gives peace. He is The One! It's clear and simple. No hustle. No bustle. No waiting. Overcoming through The Overcomer.

In one of the most amazing Christmas parties of all time, the angels announced the incredible gift of peace. "Glory to God in the highest heaven, and peace on earth to people He favors!" (Luke 2:14 HCSB).

Party Favor

It's a peace bigger than freedom from hustling/bustling—though it can definitely bring peace there. But this is a universe-sized peace that reconciles a sinful people to a holy God. Christmas is the blessed reminder that we are "people He favors"—and He favors us with His peace. Glory!

Peace with God. And peace, even rest, in our Christmas. We don't have to wait in line for this, my friends. As the old hymn in all its incarnations urged us, we can rest in God—a merry rest, for sure. Because Jesus was born. "God rest ye merry, gentlemen, Let nothing you dismay, Remember Christ our Savior was born on Christmas Day." You have to love a Christmas hymn that packages "rest" and "merry."

The Wonder of It All

I don't mind reminding us again and again—maybe even again—that it's key here to remember Christ, our overcoming Savior, the one who was born to bring peace. It's in that remembering that we find we can keep our vision crystal clear. No blurring as we trade the noisy Christmas rush for a reverent Christmas hush. It's a quiet rest we can experience, even in a not-so-silent night. Yes, even when all is downright loud. It's in that place we express—truly express—our celebration of, gratitude for, worship of, love for our Jesus.

Ah, there's the wonder. And the sweetness. Plums or no plums.

So go ahead. Line up. Ready, set—express it! And may I say, for this kind of express line, I'm all in.

Lord, may I never lose sight of the wonder of You. Keep me mindful. Keep my vision clear, I ask, when it comes to the astounding wonder, the utter beyond-my-imagination miracle, of You, my great and mighty God, being born as a baby. Jesus, oh the wonder that You would come to this planet with Your mind and heart set on the Cross. On me. On redeeming me. The wonder, my Savior. Such wonder.

Merry and Bright from Beth

Christmas lines can wear on you. I just left the loooongest line, and if you're the mom who has a toddler throwing a tantrum in checkout lane 5? The one who dug an unwrapped candy cane from the bottom of your purse and sucked the fuzz off of it *before* you plugged your two-year-old's mouth with it...well, you will OVERCOME! Although, there's no amount of love that makes purse fuzz go down any easier. But terrible twos and Christmas too, fly so fast and furious. And fuzzy. Enjoy this sweet holiday. Also, keep extra candy canes in your purse, just in case.

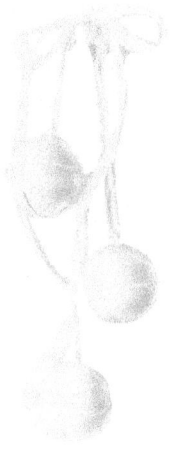

Chapter 16

Make More Room for This Christmas

Beth

"And she gave birth to her firstborn son and wrapped him in swaddling clothes and laid him in a manger, because there was no room for them in the inn" (Luke 2:7).

Just so you know, I woke up early this morning worried that you all would not be ready for Christmas. Just in case you don't have time to fret—I am prepared to worry in advance for you.

I fall for it every holiday. At night, mostly. In need of sleep, my brain entices me to instead crowd around a little announcer-voice calling, *There's plenty to see here,* and I binge-watch some old favorites. Like: "Did someone water the Christmas tree?" and "The stocking stuffers aren't even!" Then there's the rehash of the typical trope, "All the Christmas gifts I bought are lame." I really don't want to see *those* reruns again, but my brain dictates the episodes I view and never seems inclined to hand over the remote.

Last Christmas, for instance, a very awake middle-of-the-night-me tried to do some Christmas shopping online. No lines—just the power of presents at the touch of my fingertips. Only … a few of my gift ideas were a touch off. This is exactly why you shouldn't worry or shop at two a.m. You should sleep. As it turns out, grippy slippies were *not* on my husband's Christmas list. Sigh. *All the Christmas gifts I bought are lame.*

Proof that there is precious little shiny in the middle of the night(s) before Christmas. There's so much space taken up by fret and worry. We can feel like we don't have enough real estate left over to give the good things room.

Cutting Out the Complicated

Seriously. Every year I resolve to manage myself better. I insist I'll shut down the crazy Christmassing. All the traffic and people and glitter and clutter. There can be too much shoved onto one tiny space on the calendar. And you really gotta wonder why we work so hard to make more out of an already awesome event.

Like the time I insisted on baking cutout cookies from scratch with my kids. All afternoon we measured and mixed. We sifted and floured until the dog left powdery paw prints on the floor. The kids took turns wearing my handed down lime-green apron. Finally, favorite cookie cutters in hand, each child was ready to go. But the dough was not.

In human error, I'd overlooked the part of the recipe that required an overnight stay in the fridge. *When did cookies get so complicated?* So, the dough went in—the lime-green apron came off.

The next day, we baked the very complex cookies. They tasted like freezer burn so we threw them away. I scratched another attempt and bought ready-made cookies instead. That's when I discovered: my three didn't give a lick whose recipe they licked off their tiny fingers. They just sincerely enjoyed the playful, untidy time together. "Can we make some footprints in the flour again?" was all Josh cared about. Under all the commotion, it was really that simple—I'm the one who made it so hard. The fuss and extra effort. The overwhelmed. Every bit of it totally manufactured by the complicated me.

Not just in my parent-life, but also in my life-life, I feel like it's my job to add the sparkle to the season. And I love this part. I love spending time with family and friends. Baking cookies with the kids and watching the same holiday movie for the 50th time together. But then, lists squeeze. Stress crowds. Worry hoards. From the moment I wake up in the morning (or the middle of the night), I leave little space for thoughts about Jesus to spread out.

Making Room for Who Matters

All my fabricated standards magnify my production and downplay Jesus' perfection. Scripture tells us Christ's birth is meant to be celebrated the other way around.

"And she gave birth to her firstborn son and wrapped him in swaddling clothes and laid him in a manger, because there was no room for them in the inn" (Luke 2:7). I can't tell you how many times I've wrestled thoughts like: *What was the innkeeper thinking? Didn't he know how important Jesus is? See the star? Just consider helping a young couple out?* A quick glance at my calendar and I become aware of a certain solidarity with this story. I wonder if the innkeeper didn't think at all, he just reacted to the crowded day. And sometimes I do too.

I cannot tell you the amount of times I project my thoughts and feelings of "I'm not doing enough … not spending enough … not enjoying enough" onto Christmas. I mean, I let worry keep me up all night shopping for slippy socks. Which may be something you don't do, and I think my family would agree, it's just me.

We experience such easiness at Christmas when we ponder what's important, don't we?

That's why I love how these verses in Luke help unclutter my mind. "And all they that heard it wondered at those things which were told them by the shepherds. But Mary kept all these things and pondered them in her heart" (Luke 2:18-19 NKJV). Here we get this effortless glance at Mary's faith. We have the Biblical hindsight to see Mary had plenty of things to think about. To worry about and chew on at two a.m. But she chose to think about the truth of Jesus and keep only "these things."

Keep Only These Things

Mary chose to think about all that she knew to be true about God. And all the shepherds had related to her. This verse reminds us that other people wondered while Mary pondered. Mary weighed the truth of what she knew against the fear of what could be. She weighed who she was with God's worth. She had calm in Christ. Isn't it a beautiful thing that keeping our thoughts on Jesus gives us room in our heads, and in our hearts, to stretch out and breathe? Evidence faith is more than spiritual and physical, but mindful too.

Think about it. Knowing what is important to keep and think about makes us willing to let everything else go. "She kept all these things" and made room for what mattered most.

We aren't meant to just *manage* the manger—but eagerly think about who the manger held. I'm so thankful God isn't like me in what He demands from us. In what He considers to be enough. And like any one of us this year, I'm looking forward to celebrating something good and effortless. Not something overly complicated. I want to celebrate like Mary. Think like her too.

I'm learning the solid difference between the ease of contemplation and the work of worry. Also, enjoying the real and attainable thoughtfulness of the season. We can throw out stress and worry, and clear enough space to keep what *these things* are. And I don't know, just a guess here, but they probably are *not* grippy socks.

Jesus, You deserve all the space. All the room as thoughts of You take up every bit of my heart. More than once, your earthly mother took time to treasure "all these things in her heart." I miss out on so much when I work and worry and overlook the perfect gift of who You are. Keep me from fixating on outcomes while I force the little things to become the big deals. Help me consider and truly celebrate You. Purposefully. Easily. Mindfully. I'm completely overwhelmed with the truth of all the things about You, Father, yet, there is such comfort in Your righteousness, strength, and power. When I stray to do things my own way this season, draw me ever closer to You. Amen.

A Thrill of Hope from Rhonda

A million yeses to this. Maybe more. Because it's easy for me, too, to try to do things my own busy way, and to fill up all the spaces with the slippery things that don't really count. I want to think in much more of a Mary direction and "treasure." I want to remember as well to pray this prayer with Beth, giving every place—every trace of every space— to the mighty King of Grace. Out with the stress and worry. In with the Jesus-filled spaces. Ahhhh. Sleep in heavenly peace.

Chapter 17

Season's Meatings

Rhonda

"But first and most importantly seek (aim at, strive after) His kingdom and His righteousness [His way of doing and being right—the attitude and character of God], and all these things will be given to you also" (Matthew 6:33 AMP).

You know how I can tell we're approaching the Christmas season? I find myself thumbing through a catalog. A catalog. Of. *Meat.*

Potted meat. Pickled meat. Fried and dried and some on the side meat. Maybe even poached meat. That takes us only to about page five. Then there's meat by the log. Meat in a bar. Meat on a stick. Meat in a jar. And okay, that might sound a little Dr. Seuess-y-cutesy, but I get halfway through the catalog and I have to tell you, I'm pretty much meated out.

So here we are, smack-dab into the season in which we really can end up meeting ourselves coming and going. And we can also end up *meating* ourselves coming and going. Beefing it up in every way. More and more calories. More and more busyness. More.

More Than Meats the Eye

There's wisdom in keeping an eye out for the "more." Sneaky clutter can fill our stomachs, our schedules—our lives. Do you need this reminder as often as I do? Because I think I need it more. And then more. The sneaky, cluttery kind of "more" is the kind that can steal our focus from what's important. It does it by rushing us to the busyness of what's immediate instead of waiting for the blessedness of what's vital.

We tend to think of ourselves as mature followers of Christ as long as we're not throwing big-baby fits. But maturity includes so much more than that. It includes making wise choices—with our resources, with our time, with our focus. Let's face it, some of us make more big-baby-choices during a holiday season than we do any other time of the year.

How can we be grown up about our "more"? The answer is: Jesus. Glorious Jesus. Our Triune God, "the only God, our Savior, through Jesus Christ our Lord, be glory, majesty, dominion, and authority, before all time and now and forever" (Jude 25). We grow up into our more by taking our eyes off our own schedules and wants and everything fleshy. Eyes off me. Eyes on Christ. It was because of selfish fleshliness that Paul said the Christians in Corinth couldn't have solid spiritual food. "I was not able to speak to you as spiritual people but as people of the flesh, as babies in Christ … because you are still fleshly" (1 Corinthians 3:1, 3 HCSB). He said in verse 2, "I gave you milk to drink, not solid food." Put away the catalogs, Corinthians. No meat for you.

Hungry for the Right Kind of Wisdom

Paul warns later in that same passage that "No one should deceive himself. If anyone among you thinks he is wise in this age, he must become foolish so that he can become wise. For the wisdom of this world is foolishness with God" (1 Corinthians 3:18-19 HCSB).

It's sad to get caught up in the shopping and the busyness and the more shopping and more busyness, thinking we're accomplishing works of value, then discover we've been foolishly lying to ourselves about what's important the whole time.

The psalmist puts it this way. "Why is everyone hungry for more? 'More, more,' they say. 'More, more.' I have God's more-than-enough, More joy in one ordinary day Than they get in all their shopping sprees. At day's end I'm ready for sound sleep, For you, GOD, have put my life back together" (Psalm 4:6-8 The Message).

We need a wisdom-inducing Jesus-reminder every single step along the way as we navigate the season. Have you ever thought about the fact that on that first Christmas, there was no shopping? Weird thought, isn't it? The good news of great joy the angel announced to the shoppers ... I mean ... the shepherds ... was the amazing news of the Savior's birth. What an amazing story we find in Luke 2:8-11. "In the same region, shepherds were staying out in the fields and keeping watch at night over their flock. Then an angel of the Lord stood before them, and the glory of the Lord shone around them, and they were terrified. But the angel said to them, 'Don't be afraid, for look, I proclaim to you good news of great joy that will be for all the people: Today a Savior, who is Messiah the Lord, was born for you in the city of David'" (HCSB).

Keeping Watch for Wisdom

Keeping watch over their catalogs for meat? Keeping watch over the sales by newspaper? Nah. Whatever we're watching, may we remember that it's really all about Jesus our King. Praise God the Father for the history-rocking, eternity-locking birth of the King. What a wonder that he came, knowing the cost of our salvation would be his very life. Nothing can compare with the purchase He made for us—the purchase of our eternity. The price: the blood of Jesus.

Our salvation is only found in Him. The wisdom we need is also only found in Jesus. It's time to put away that self-deceived baby stuff and sink our teeth into some meat. As we seek the Lord, He will give us the wisdom and direction we need to sort out our to-do's. It's only in Him that our choices can count. It's only in Him that we're able to identify the foolish temporary and then trade it for the will of God. We don't need that other kind of "more." We only need more Jesus.

That's exactly what will make our season, well, *more*. But more in every good way. More in ways we can see and in ways we can't. It's more than meets the eye. You might even say … it's more than *meats* the eye.

> *More You, Jesus. Less me. Less stuff. Less empty business. Less of the foolish fancies of the world. Please give me more You. I want to seek You first, before I head anywhere else. I ask that You would grant me the wisdom I need for this day, and everything else to boot. By Your grace and mercy, lead me in making right choices. Let me grow up in You, Lord. More and more and more.*

Merry and Bright from Beth

Rhonda, this hits HOME! It's also hard for a doer to hear. With every pain suffered, my natural tendency is to settle for my less rather than seek God's more. Funny, too, God's Word never directs me to rely more on myself, go more with my gut, work more to forgive, or seek more stuff. God sustains and *meets* me with His power of renewal, refreshment, and substantial wisdom. Seems I'm happier to be a work in progress when I stay faithful to His process. And because He meets us right where we are, we can enjoy the process even more this Christmas.

Chapter 18

Something Stocking Stuffers

Beth

"He must increase, but I must decrease"
(John 3:30).

The stocking stuffers aren't even even. This is just one of the casually catastrophic thoughts I can have at midnight on Christmas Eve.

What happened? When did stuffing a sock become my thing to think about? And why do I spend all the extra mental energy trying to discover why packaged bows don't stick? For me, getting those things to stay is like trying to apply magnetic eyelashes. Sticky bows could be a try-to-get-them-to-stick science fair experiment (a blue ribbon one at that). Or they could be wrapped in the same package as the not-so-outdoor outdoor Christmas light conspiracy. Really, why don't twinkle lights ever seem to work past Christmas? Does that happen to everyone, or just here in the Midwest? Or maybe … it's just me.

My husband credits human error. One Christmas we took extra effort to put our lights away. Jerry encouraged, *Wrap them loosely. Untangle them gently. Hold them carefully. Lightly. And slightly off the ground.* We did all of this. Only none of them worked the following year. Ugh.

And so I wasn't super surprised to read an article that said 88 percent of people report pre-Christmas-preparation stress. And I suppose our ever-growing, off-to-working song of "stuff the stockings, make the bows, kill the lights," well … none of that helps either. There is just so much stuff.

For instance, last year I decided to simplify. I partially emptied and tried like mad to declutter my Christmas containers. I got approximately nowhere. Because when I returned from my Christmas-excess-jettisoning mission and witnessed how much remained, I realized I'd hardly made a dent. All the containers were still so overstuffed. Somehow. All I can say is we're like really, really into Christmas.

Uncluttered

Anyway. I tried to give the surplus of decorations to my children, but (in a surprising show of sibling solidarity) they all crowded firmly into the same camp, under a banner of "We plan to do Christmas a lot simpler than you do, Mom. We don't want to overdo." Oh. Well, then.

Obviously, my plan was to have to compose a fair system to divvy out all the stuff, even while I worried that their stockings weren't stuffed evenly. So their response threw me. Why? Why don't they want my stuff? And really #whosekidsarethese, anyway?

Their point made sense, though. And by the looks of my superfluous everything, I sorta expected I'd naturally raised similarly tinsel-hoarding children. But they seemed to somehow have picked up along the way that it really is important to be mindful of what we add in and what we take away. Especially at Christmas. Simple can be good.

Last week, my best friend and I wandered into an adorable tea-room for lunch. The place had all the linens and plates and pines and a tiny dish with a baby-sized spoon in the center of our table. *Fancy.* So I ordered tea and lobbed extra-tiny teaspoons of white into my cup with both my fancy fingers pointed to the sky.

Small detail: It's good to know what *exactly* it is that you've extra'd into your tea, or you may hand it back to the server explaining, *"My tea tastes like the ocean. Sorry."* Ah, these mishaps push me toward Jesus. Because things can go from fancy to fallen real fast!

Hold the Extra

I suppose when you're such an over-thinker, over-decorator, over-doer, and extra-adder, going overboard with anything else is no surprise. Because it's easy to function from the thought of scarcity and not from plenty. That's just how strong the sin of "this is not enough" works. We can heap the wrong things and think life will taste just a tiny-dish sweeter when we do. Honestly, there is something infinitely healing in the thought that—unlike sugar or salt (*label the dishes, please, fancy people*)—there is nothing I can add to the simple joys of Christmas.

Decluttering is tough when you're the mom who thinks she has to pack it all in. Over prepare. You have the big purse with the pudding snacks, the band aids, the extra pair of gloves. Even on vacation this past summer, you stuff six cans of sunscreen (no joke), into a suitcase and two bottles of aloe. Just in case. If this is you, too, you know why exactly Christmas can be such a catch-all for more. And why it's important to simplify.

More than that—I do crave more of Jesus at Christmastime.

Simplify the Season

When I create a season revolving around so much extra, I forget that Jesus humbled Himself as a servant for less. Less perfect. Less worship. Less love. Less holy. Rather than coming first as a King and our God, He came to us as a lowly baby.

The expectations of the world were so misguided, people looked for a ruler, not a Redeemer. But an angel said, "I'm here to announce a great and joyful event that is meant for everybody, worldwide: A Savior has been born in David's town … This is what you look for: a baby wrapped in a blanket and lying in a manger" (Luke 2:10-12 The Message). This story is evergreen. The shepherds had nothing to bring the King except themselves. As ones chosen and amazed, they hurried humbly there. The lowest members of society, they show up with … nothing.

And Scripture reminds us just how low Jesus was willing to go. How much more He was willing to offer. "And being found in human form, he humbled himself by becoming obedient to the point of death, even death on a cross" (Philippians 2:8). The message of a lowly baby's birth given to the lowly humble shepherds. We can only imagine the gravity of this gift. The infallible to the fallen. On purpose! This gift is still so amazing, with the same humble reminder…we are not worthy. But He is. We show up as we are asked to: empty-handed.

Full to Overflowing

When we humble ourselves and allow God to carry it all—when we celebrate Christmas through the eyes of less—we can see how much more we've been given. Not only is less this Christmas a relief, it's renovating in the simplest way possible. On the flip side, less of everything else means more energy to give away.

But the only way to get more of Jesus is to get more of Jesus. Extra of His Word. Extra of who He is. His story is real and provisional, powerful. Then—and only then—will we experience a refreshment and enthusiasm we aren't responsible for. The gracious kind that demonstrates grace and mercy, and the reason we get to celebrate at all.

He came to offer more. More joy, more peace, more life than what this world has to offer. What an uncluttered thought, that His love is enough. And we can enjoy every bit of Christmas that God has given.

It's renovating to proclaim that Jesus was born! Even more life changing to live like we truly believe He lived!

You can try to judge a moment for all that it lacks, but so much more life is lived when you notice all that it doesn't. We don't have to bemoan the broken lights. The added stuff. We can even ignore when the stockings aren't even. *Forget about it.* He will overstuff the stockings with blessings anyhow.

So, hold the extra! Especially the extra *fancy* salt. Hold that, yes.

Father, You are over and above enough. Forgive me for the times I've shown up with my arms full and ready to impress. For the times I've allowed my inverted pride to push me to do more, be more, and try to accomplish more, all while my heart insinuates You are less. I try to make the lights work and stuff all the stuff. It leaves me empty. I adore You, Jesus. You alone.

Thrill of Hope from Rhonda

Ah, the magic of Christmas un-lights. You get one season. Just one season. That's it. As we look heart-ward, though, let's let the season stay fully lit. Why settle for one season? It would be like settling for salt tea when we could have it deliciously sweetened. The biggest question of all is, why would we ever want to settle for a mere ruler when we can have a Redeemer? A ruler might sort out some of the issues of our here and now. Even that's a big maybe. But a Redeemer? A Redeemer for-sure settles our eternity. That's a forever shining truth that will put the biggest, most enthusiastic hallelujah in every part of our Christmas.

Chapter 19

Fruitcake—You Are What You Eat

Rhonda

"With all my heart I have sought You, [inquiring of You and longing for You]; Do not let me wander from Your commandments [neither through ignorance nor by willful disobedience]. Your word I have treasured and stored in my heart, That I may not sin against You. Blessed and reverently praised are You, O Lord; Teach me Your statutes" (Psalm 119:10-12 AMP).

've met a lot of people in my lifetime. Thousands, I'd say. Tens of thousands for all I know. And of all those people, the number who like the taste of fruitcake? About four. I know one family that still gets a fruitcake from a relative every year. Not to be ugly, but I think they sometimes use it to level the tree.

Another friend of mine told me that their family waits for the fruitcake gifts to come in when they're short a bookend or two. I didn't figure out that she was joshing me about that particular DIY until she told me that those bookends also keep bugs away. That silly friend.

If you're one of the four, please forgive me for everything I've just said (I've noticed you four people can be very defensive and also very intense about your fervent love for fruitcake).

One of the four once told me it's all in how you make your fruitcake. Make? Bake? As in, cook and/or create it? Then it's for sure all over for me.

Unpacking the Fruitcake

I know I make a lot of jokes about my making/baking/cooking/creating skills. It's hard not to. There's just a lot of material there. But every once in a while, I do like to put something together in my own kitchen. It's not fruitcake, of course. And also, for me, it's more like a game show than it is cooking. I pick the right boxes, and then I sort of "win" dinner. *Let's make a meal!* Pick this cardboard boxed food to go with that cardboard boxed food. I know you're tempted to judge me harshly right about now. I wish I could think of a reason you shouldn't.

If you're not judging because you're also a "boxer," let me warn you. If you read a package label or two, you could experience some distress. Last time I read labels on a couple of my handy-dandy, put-em-together-in-ten-minutes boxes, I noticed the ingredients read almost exactly like the list of ingredients on my shampoo bottle. What *is* that stuff? Chemicals. Preservatives. More chemicals. I didn't know if I should "heat and serve" or "lather, rinse, repeat."

I hear a lot of people talk about how it's probably healthier to chuck the contents and eat the boxes instead. Those boxes are made of cardboard. Which is made from trees. Trees are plants. So I'm thinking … vegetable.

Hey, with a nice sauce that could be a viable option. I'd call it thinking outside the box, dinner-wise, except that in this scenario I'm still pretty committed to the box. For the record, yes, I do realize I could stand to get a little more committed to nutrition and a little less committed to boxes. Also maybe more fruit, less cake.

Boxed In—And Also Out

And while I can joke all day about dinner and all its colorful box choices, I want you to know I take spiritual nourishment altogether seriously. I'm committed.

The psalmist prayed, "I will meditate on Your precepts and think about Your ways. I will delight in Your statutes; I will not forget Your word" (Psalm 119:15-16 HCSB). He got it. In verse 5 of that same chapter, he ponders as he prays, "If only my ways were committed to keeping Your statutes!"

Some days the schedule is so crazy I wonder how I can possibly squeeze in time in God's word. Those are the days it makes no sense not to. Absolutely no sense. That commitment has to kick in full on. How can I make all the snap decisions and handle the extra stresses of a busy day without being equipped—fed spiritually—through spending time in His word? A busy day is not a day we want to spend struggling against spiritual malnourishment.

We stay physically fit as we seek closeness with the Father and as we seek to sync our mind to His. Sync our heart to His. If we check the passage at the top of this chapter, we're reminded that we're not truly, wholeheartedly seeking if we're ignoring His message to us via His word. "With all my heart I have sought You [inquiring of You and longing for You]; Do not let me wander from Your commandments [neither through ignorance nor by willful disobedience]" (Psalm 119:10 AMP).

Hey, want some delicious blessing and favor? How about this for the best dessert: "Blessed and favored by God are those who keep His testimonies, And who [consistently] seek Him and long for Him with all their heart" (Psalm 119:2 AMP). Blessing and favor—the cherry on top!

Tick All the Right Boxes

There's no meal, inside or outside the box, that satisfies like time with the Lord. "You satisfy me as with rich food; my mouth will praise You with joyful lips" (Psalm 63:5 HCSB). And nevermind all those preservatives in my box dinners. As we seek the Lord, our *souls* are preserved. "The Lord shall preserve you from all evil; He shall preserve your soul," (Psalm 121:7 NKJV).

Staying in His word joyfully nourishes my soul in the most preservative direction. And I will remain … committed.

You might be interested to know that while I will not remain all that committed to my boxed preservatives, since those chemicals are engineered for the express purpose of making things last longer, I'm still thinking I should live to be about 342.

Father, thank You that You didn't leave me here without instructions. Thank You for the direction You provide in Your word. Teach me by it. Teach me to treasure it. Remind me that every time I seek Your word, I'm seeking You, and lead me to seek with my whole heart. Lead me in reading it, internalizing it, meditating on it, learning by it—being changed by it. Lord, let it be my food—like the sweetest dessert. May it strengthen me, keep me from sin; all glory to You.

Merry and Bright from Beth

Did you know the U.S. Department of *Agriculture* (huh?) says that fruitcake will last up to 2-3 months? And frozen? Maybe forever. For a culture that likes our food fast, we sure do like it to last. But even the greatest preservatives won't outlast this life. There are two eternal things in this world: our souls and God's Word. Our concept of eternity is a pivotal force in how much hope we have in this day—in how much hope we feel at Christmas. With Jesus, our celebration isn't tinsel and temporary, but the gift that lasts forever. And ever. Even beyond fruitcake!

Chapter 20

Deck the Walls

Beth

"Then I said, 'I will appeal to this, to the years of the right hand of the Most High.' I will remember the deeds of the Lord; yes, I will remember your wonders of old. I will ponder all your work" (Psalm 77:10-12a).

'm not one to whitewash the current day, but squinting hard to see the good in it isn't a bad idea either. Although, there's just some life decor you can't unsee.

For instance, there was a season when my daughter was very ill. And our family dog was anxious. Also the bowl of jello wasn't set yet. The long story, cut to the size of a one-inch Christmas ribbon—our dog knocked a bowl of red gelatin out of our sick daughter's hands during a zoomy rampage through the house. The jello fa-la-la-la-landed all over the wall and left a permanent stain. Believe it or not, if I squint,

I can still see the small red tint peeking through the white wall. *Deck the walls with bowls of jello...* plays on a loop in my head. Every time.

The thing is, that Christmas was a difficult time for our family, yet I couldn't allow the trials we suffered dampen the thrill of what Christmas could be: decorated with joy. Also, jello.

I can't say I anticipated everything would go all right. But I also refused to believe everything would go wrong. Still, in the words of Mr. Rogers, "There are times when explanations, no matter how reasonable, just don't seem to help." It is within those times we can choose God to bring the loving comfort we need.

There is no life free of pain—and so we live in the middle of quiet hope. We daydream of a haystall and lambs that sleep silently while Jesus slept sound.

Maybe this year for you is less jolly and more *jello*. But just listen to this wonderful Scripture from the Psalms. "I waited patiently for the Lord to help me and he turned to me and heard my cry" (Psalm 40:1 NLT). Seasonal discouragement can sneak up on you. But God's head turns towards you.

We Can Be Jolly with Jello

It's true though, sometimes when you're feeling comfy, BOOM! There's a painful surprise. It makes it tough to stay positive. Especially this time of year. All the anticipation (for good or for not-so) can dampen our spirits. You may even wonder if God sees your discomfort. Or if He cares.

But those harder discouragements can drive us deeper with God. For instance, a few months ago I killed an orange traffic barrel on I-77, or so I thought. After hitting it, I glanced in my mirror to see it stand back up again.

Like it was waving at me.

The next ten miles were filled with dread and debate. I really didn't even want to see the mess I'd made of the car. Then I stopped, and there it was: discouragement. It may have looked like a jolly candy cane stripe down the length of my white Jeep—I knew better. Instead of jolly, it brought with it something I'd recognize anywhere. That sense of dread that shows up with the resilience of a pop-back-up construction barrel. Disappointment can really leave a mark. And girls, it doesn't die without a fight. Take it from me—frustration works hard to deck our walls. But we *can* be jolly with jello.

It Goes from Good to Really Good

We can feel it in our heart, in our home. We see it. The mood of "not enough" that can ensue. That joyless space in the middle of conflict or uncertainty. The out-of-place red something that still shows through. But we can still approach Christmas with wide-eyed wonder and anticipation. Let's not forget how unimaginative the enemy is. He uses despair; he throws the jello, he stations roadblocks to make us forget: God cares.

If you have 99 problems, you can trust God is working in all of them. You can own the thought that God works for good in what looks bad to you. We can't let our hearts be ruled by what we see. Or don't.

Deck it Out!

We have to trust the truth of God's plan through every disappointment life brings. Knowing He has declared, "my thoughts are not your thoughts, neither are your ways my ways" (Isaiah 55:8 NIV). The manger scene? More proof that, in all God's ways, He shines a light on His glory, not ours. With His eternal effort, He changes our bad to His good. The way God is, plans, purposes, and provides gives our souls room to spread out. To believe. We have the hope we need for the amazing story of what lies ahead.

Not only does God care—He's there. His love is with us. David prayed, "Where shall I go from your Spirit? Or where shall I flee from your presence? If I ascend to heaven, you are there! If I make my bed in Sheol, you are there! If I take the wings of the morning and dwell in the uttermost parts of the sea, even there your hand shall lead me, and your right hand shall hold me" (Psalm 139:7-10). You can't cover up the enthusiasm here—or the faith to fight difficulty with truth. It would have been easy for David to fold up his mat and go home, but David knew that where he was, God was. In a sense, David trusted God to adorn his life perfectly.

It would have been easy for Mary to say no. For the wise men not to follow. For the shepherds to remain in the field. But ... *your right hand shall hold me.*

The Maker's Gonna Make Something Great

The Christmas story reminds us that God's love is extreme. He refreshes us when we're extremely overwhelmed. Comforts when we're more than tired. Encourages us always. Because let's read verse 8 again. Hell to heaven, there is no place or thing or circumstance that overextends or out-reaches God's hand.

Jesus showed us how to live here on earth. He prayed, He sought, He submitted to God's right hand of authority. He surrendered to joy and the white space of comfort.

And maybe you've never thought of fighting this way: by not fighting. Maybe instead, you battle hard and sleep restless. You kick the tire. Discouragement happens most when we try to handle life's disappointments our way and give up rather than settle in. God wants us to hand it over. All the jello, all the streaks, all the mess. He has a great plan for renovation. Sometimes it's even a total redo, but you can rely on this truth: The Maker is restoring love, joy, forgiveness...in the hardest parts of your life. You will not be disappointed.

Need encouragement? You'll run into it when you take time to think of all the work God's doing. Right now. You just can't shovel any new feelings of hope in fast enough to keep up with God.

So, let the joy and jello fa-la-la-la-fall where they may. Although next time, I do sorta, kinda hope it's not on my wall!

Father, help me submit to You. To Your will. To Your love and comfort. In every situation, You never leave me. What a joy it is to surrender to You. Please keep me trusting You for all the strength to battle less. In Jesus' name, Amen.

Thrill of Hope from Rhonda

I'm so glad that jolly doesn't stain like Jello. But Beth is right that both can leave a mark. She's right on as well with her reminder that in joy or sorrow—and in mixes of both—our Father is at work. I love the encouragement in this chapter to guard against letting our hearts be ruled by what we see. Or by what we don't see. We can ever trust that He is there and that He cares. What a mighty God we serve. What a glorious Jesus we celebrate.

Chapter 21

Don't Flake Out

Rhonda

"As for God, His way is blameless. The word of the LORD is tested [it is perfect, it is faultless]; He is a shield to all who take refuge in Him. For who is God, but the LORD? Or who is a rock, except our God, The God who encircles me with strength And makes my way blameless? He makes my feet like hinds' feet [able to stand firmly and tread safely on paths of testing and trouble]; He sets me [securely] upon my high places"
(Psalm 18:30-33 AMP).

Looking for an idea for a holiday craft project that's out of the ordinary? One that's not for the faint of heart? Think about ice sculpting. Have you seen some of those amazing sculptures? I am altogether wowed by the art people create out of plain old everyday frozen water. It's a topper for me that the artists don't even seem ruffled that their works of art aren't going to stay frozen. Eventually that sculpture will be a puddle. Definitely not your basic DIY.

If you need a great conversation starter at your Christmas party, plant yourself a Frosty the Snowman ice sculpture smack in the middle of your party table. I want to say that it makes a great icebreaker, but I also don't want to say it. That Frosty is a work of art, so please don't break him. I think it would also be an interesting and layered meta message, what with Frosty puddling out around the end of the party.

So yes, I'll just keep coming up with the ideas. You guys can make them happen. I've settled comfortably into a role as an idea person, and not so much the artist/crafty/createy/makey-bakey person. And hold on, because this idea person just got a doozy of a new idea. Instead of ice, we could go with ice *cream*. Now there's a Christmas party centerpiece I would circle around. And around. With a spoon. I could talk about that sculpture all night long. Icebreaker done.

I'm Cooking Up Another Idea

Hey, while I'm DIY idea-storming, hear me out on this one. A club sandwich, only all zillion layers are ice cream. Ice cream on ice cream on ice cream. Best ice cream sandwich ever, right?

Seems like it would make sense right here to introduce the idea of an ice cream club. The first rule of ice cream club would have to be that you never talk about the calories in ice cream club.

It's still better that I cook up ideas instead of trying to cook up anything … you know … edible. I remember trying to fix something new for dinner now and then when my children were growing up. I think we've already established and re-re-established that I'm not a cook. Let me say that no one knows better than my kids. Our family's reminiscing often goes like this:

"Hey Mom. Remember that time you were trying a new recipe and then you found the word 'blanch' in it? So you poured us all a bowl of cereal instead?"

Oh yes, I do. I do remember. It probably snap-crackle-saved-their-lives.

Believing with Every Fiber of My Being

On the topic of cereal, have you ever noticed that you can go eight months without eating any breakfast cereal at all? Eight months. And then suddenly you find yourself compelled to have it? To have *six bowls* of it. Probably at midnight. Let me believe this happens to you too, will you?

I feel I should insert something here about my "moral fiber," but the idea person inside me is telling me that's probably not a great idea.

Anytime I've caught myself wrestling with the too-much-midnight-cereal compulsion, however, I've tried to remind myself that over-fibering at midnight doesn't always make for the best night's sleep. Eventually, I remember.

The Key Ingredient

There's a recipe of faith, of sorts, that's so much better to remember. It's more than just an idea. It's a vital fact of faith. Have you ever encountered someone who started out with enthusiastic joy in the Lord, but then got easily tripped up or sidetracked? Anyone who doesn't understand and remember this one crucial element of the walk of faith will find the entire structure of their spirit melting in a blanched-out snap, crackle, squash. That key ingredient? An accurate understanding, and a consistent remembering, of the true character of God.

It's not possible to over-emphasize how critical it is to understand, believe, remember God's character if we're going to follow Him well. Is there anything more imperative than knowing—like, soul-level knowing—that He is trustworthy? Think about it. How could any of us possibly consider surrendering to and following a God we can't trust? How could we ever worship someone who is not worthy of our worship?

Following Him devotedly makes sense when we remember who He is and see Him as He is. Our God is good, and He is holy. He is kind and loving. We can trust that there's never anything He doesn't know. All that goodness is wrapped up in power. That makes trust in Him well-placed and connection with Him sweet. And, miracle of miracles, He desires that connection with us. He longs to show us more of Himself. Second Chronicles 16:9 tells us, "the eyes of the Lord roam throughout the earth to show himself strong for those who are wholeheartedly devoted to him" (CSB).

Follow This Recipe

To know Him by name—that is, personally—leads to a place of wholehearted, devoted trust. "Those who know your name trust in you" (Psalm 9:10 CSB). It's a place of loving fellowship—with a natural and flourishing outflow of worship.

As we study Him and spend time with Him, we understand more and more that He is worthy of our worship, worthy of our devotion, worthy of our trust. And I think it blesses Him when we remember, know, and trust. When we reminisce often. Moment by moment. Layer by layer. I would compare the layers to the most delicious ice cream club sandwich here, but remembering, knowing, and trusting is infinitely bigger, better, sweeter.

So let me remind you even now, that He is worthy of your devotion. Know Him. He desires that. Follow Him. It's the faith recipe for the most gloriously worthwhile life. "Know that the Lord your God is God, the faithful God who keeps his gracious covenant loyalty for a thousand generations with those who love him and keep his commands" (Deuteronomy 7:9 CSB).

Ah, the life of trusting a trustworthy God. It's almost unimaginably wonderful. Practically surreal. If not cereal.

On the more surface side, this entire ice sculpture/ice cream sandwich/fiber/cereal conversation has been filled with some of my best ideas. And they all circle around and connect. Snowflakes. Bran flakes. Frosty. Frosted flakes. I could keep circling, but something tells me that might be another bad idea. I should probably remember to listen better to that something.

Father, every worthy idea is from You. Every good thing, from You. Help me remember that. Lead me in daily remembering who You are. I'm intentionally remembering in this very moment that You are good, You are holy, You are kind, You are loving, You are all-knowing, You are all-powerful, You are completely trustworthy. Give me a consistent and accurate understanding and remembering of Your perfect character. Thank You that You are worthy of my worship. I worship You even now. In the name of Jesus, my Savior.

Merry and Bright from Beth

All this connecting reminds me of a recent room renovation. Would you believe it all started with replacing a light switch that was *flaky*? The project just got bigger from there. Such is our faith. A day-to-day-knowing-God-more faith starts with reliance and grows. Because God doesn't change. We do. Get this? Our bigger faith sees a bigger God. A God who can handle our worries and can change our lives. Rhonda, I'm so thankful for all these powerful connections. Your wisdom. Your words. And also, your suggestion of an ice cream club. This might be your best idea yet!

Chapter 22

Home Sweet Home

Beth

"For every house is built by someone, but the builder of all things is God" (Hebrews 3:4).

Funny story. A few years ago I picked up a gingerbread house kit the whole family could construct. Even the extended family joined in to make this sugar-plum house a home. Because how complicated can one of these tiny houses be, right?

Turns out, crazy hard!

Taking turns, we worked on (and snacked on), and had trouble getting the house to stand up on, its own. We would let go, only to watch the walls shift and move and fall. Every time. Although it took several rebuilds before the icing cemented everything into place, we were never too sad to try again.

Can I tell you our sugary mess looked nothing like the edible mansion on the front of the box? Eh. Although you want it to look appetizing, who really eats a gingerbread house, anyway? (Aside from our dog who helped herself to the front door.) Mostly, gingerbread houses aren't for eating, they're for building. Constructing. Because creating is a primary part of the plan.

A Living House

Lately, I've considered some of the lessons I learned from that confectionary construction. Like how similar it is to the building up of delightful things in our lives. And, at the same time, how hard it can be to be patient with the build. Calm during the construction. More than that though, I've considered how God glories over the rebuild of us. He doesn't make us a house of crumbling crackers and say, "Sorry you feel weak and rundown. You sure are a fixer upper. Hang on. Eventually, I'll get to work on you." He doesn't consider us a whole-house breakdown.

No.

Without any exaggeration, Jesus felt the full burden of flesh and is the eternal power of God. A loving Rock. The cornerstone of Christmas. Even before the world knew of the celebration to take place, God showed David the blueprint. "He is the one who will build a house for my Name, and I will establish the throne of his kingdom forever. I will be his father, and he will be my son" (2 Samuel 7:13-14a NIV). Jesus Christ is the living house. And conversely, our hearts? A place He can move in and call home.

How sweet it all is to think of God patiently assembling me while I blow hot air on the icing to make everything dry *faster*! Geeze Louise, He knows me. He knows us. And the Master Builder knows what He's doing.

"God is building a home. He's using us all—irrespective of how we got here—in what he is building. He's used the apostles and prophets for the foundation. Now he's using you, fitting you in brick by brick, stone by stone, with Christ Jesus as the cornerstone that holds all parts together. We see it taking shape day after day—a holy temple built by God, all of us built into it, a temple in which God is quite at home" (Ephesians 2:20-22 The Message).

It seems everyone has their own idea of what home truly is. But this verse reminds us of God's daily effort to dwell in our hearts.

All the verbing—like using, building, fitting, and shaping—leads me to believe the noun of "temple" is the magnificent structure He has in mind. We are a whole building being built up by Him. And according to this verse, He is propelling us in a powerful way.

Although. This Christmas will pace its very own self, I think. And is it just me, or does it feel these past months were like slow motion chaos?

Extreme Home Makeover—Again

For me, possibly for you, too—it's been a hard swing between nesting and purging. Waiting and blowing. Blustering even. I look at the unopened box of Christmas cards on the counter while I work to dry the icing, all the other things on my list. Can't faith grow faster? I admit that I've held onto what I think Christmas should be. I've clung to that perfect photo on the front of the box.

Just last week, I saw a magazine with over-the-top Christmas decor on the cover. The people smiled in their renovated house surrounded by fluffy pillows and freshly picked pine. And I'm so sorry. I felt like I wanted to call a hotline. "Hello. I can barely muster the energy to keep the counter clean right now, so where can I find the enthusiasm to clean *and* decorate? *Also, how do the magazine families keep their pillows so poofy? Are my flat pillows not picture-worthy, people?*" Never mind that our Christmas tree, decorated and still *alive*, constitutes our biggest renovation this year by far.

I'm not sure what caused that manic moment, either. Because my family will say I still love to decorate for Christmas a little too much! I just think some proverbial fluff has been pulled out of our pillows. And yet, as the busy bustle has deflated, it's made Christmas feel a little fuller. And unless my perfect ideal is demolished, God can't build fresh again.

Oddly enough, I've discovered this steadying verse this season: "Unless the Lord builds the house, its builders labor in vain" (Psalm 127:1a NIV). In my gut, I can feel it—a sense that it's never too late to build on the true meaning of Christmas. To embrace the calm of Jesus in this slower chaos.

Bigger is Better

Let's drive a stake of confidence in what God is creating. Rebuilding even.

Because it's almost like He's offered the valuable gift of a remake this year. A time to cozy in with Him. It could be that there's additional space to start a new passion or career, a new relationship, or a new adventure embarking on a season of change led by an unchangeable God. Sure, we might all be a little homesick this holiday. I'm guessing we may crave the feel of Christmases past. But girl, we can get excited about what God is building. Perhaps a less fluffy, less insistent, largely simpler season? Although sometimes it's the *Just wait and see what He is creating!* The wait, it can be the hardest part.

The crazy hard part.

But let's cut the fresh pines and fluff the pillows! Remember, God is doing the work, and our celebration of Jesus is not in vain. God moves as the angel greets Mary with the announcement, "You are favored by the Lord! The Lord is with you" (Luke 1:28 GW). Then the angel delivers the news of Jesus and God's established plan. "The Holy Spirit will come to you, and the power of the most High will overshadow you" (vs. 35). What gets me is all this exciting news was followed by Mary's profound response. "May everything you have said about me come true" (vs. 38 NLT). Mary was saying, *let everything you just said happen to me.* This act of instant faith so uncomplicatedly shows the world how great a house our God can build.

The New Build

Yet I cannot think of a time I truly told God, *Let it happen.* Maybe more like, *I can make it happen.* Or *God, can You help me make it happen?* Even *Why did this happen?* Always, forever, when we trust God to do the work, the home He is making for us is so much better than any home we could wish to build ourselves. We can stand still and let God move. In.

So let's feel this release from our December performance, shall we? And capture this lightness of what God is doing. I've realized with renewed clarity a Christmas that demands less fluff will help us move more effortlessly and closer to Jesus than ever before. Maybe we work harder to lean harder. To stand firm on a God's foundation, joining Him in His work, rather than trying to make everything stand up on its very own. To spend more time with Him because He is our home sweet home.

Also, there are a few added things you should know.

1. Gingerbread houses never look like the picture on the front of the box.
2. Once constructed, a gingerbread house can last up to 3, 4, even 6 months. It petrifies like real wood.
3. This chapter is kid tasted, Mother approved.

Father, thank You for the gift of Your Son. Yes, You are my living house, forever. Continue to make me a place where You feel "quite at home," Lord. A home that is sweet for You to dwell. Teach us to stand still in Your presence. Keep us in the calm hope of what You are constructing this Christmas. And forever. Amen.

A Thrill of Hope from Rhonda

I've tried those do-it-yourself gingerbread house kits too. I totally could've snapped and pinned any one of them onto those internet spaces for hilarious fails. I probably could've gone viral more than once. Why do they even put that picture on the front of the box? There are fixer uppers and then there are those dwelling places that need a big ol' condemned notice slapped on them.

Today, though, I'm thankful beyond words that there is "no condemnation for those who are in Christ Jesus" (Romans 8:1). Because of Christ Jesus: my heart, His home. I love Beth's encouragement to "stand still and let God move. In." Home sweetest home.

Chapter 23

Yet in Thy Dark Streets Shineth

Rhonda

*"And leaving Nazareth he went and lived in Capernaum
by the sea, in the territory of Zebulun and Naphtali, so that
what was spoken by the prophet Isaiah might be fulfilled:
'The land of Zebulun and the land of Naphtali, the way of
the sea, beyond the Jordan, Galilee of the Gentiles—the people
dwelling in darkness have seen a great light, and for those
dwelling in the region and shadow of death, on them a light
has dawned'" (Matthew 4:13-16).*

O the Christmas tales I could tell. Tales of years past when the family spent more time untangling twinkle lights than we did wrapping presents. It was DIY lighting that never quite did anything. Too many times, those twinkle lights would neither twinkle nor light.

What a sad fizzle.

After the Christmas season ends, it's often not so much the lights that fizzle. It's the decorators. Or maybe moreso, the *un*-decorators.

UN-do It Yourself

I get it, OK? We have a hard time letting go of the season. I was thinking that this year we should try something different. We could try doing Christmas. And then when it's over, we could wait until next year to do Christmas again. My good friends—who also happen to be my neighbors—kept their Christmas lights up, and even the tree up, until June last year. *June!* It was so cute. They still turned the lights on every night. When summer rolled around, we were trying to decide if it was a late Christmas celebration or an early one for the next year.

When they came over for Bible study one evening, I teased them, "Tonight you will be visited by the Ghost of CHRISTMAS IS OVER, PEOPLE!"

Then again, I've heard a lot of people judge when it's time to take down the Christmas tree by how dry the tree is and/or whether or not it's currently on fire. Counting my blessings. Since my neighbor's tree is fake.

I understand how tough it can be to get motivated to take the decorations down and put them all away. Decorating? So exciting. But taking them down is rather a bummer. Last year I tried, "Okay, Google: Take down my Christmas lights," but … nothing. "Alexa, box up these ornaments." Still nothing. There really should be an app for that.

Twinkle-thinking

You know what? My neighbors might just have it right. Their twinkling tree and all the shiny lights on their house lit up our neighborhood most of the year. Maybe I'm the one who needs to adjust my thinking about what's seasonal and what's not. The truth is, my neighbors don't leave their Christmas decorations up because they're lazy about taking them down. They leave them up because they love Christmas. They really, really love Christmas.

The pre-Christmas celebrations started long before there was a first Christmas. Seven-hundred years before Christ, Isaiah wrote, "The people walking in darkness have seen a great light; a light has dawned on those living in the land of darkness" (Isaiah 9:2 CSB). Then in verse 6 he wrote, "For a child will be born to us, a son will be given to us; And the government will rest on His shoulders; And His name will be called Wonderful Counselor, Mighty God, Eternal Father, Prince of Peace" (NASB).

This? Oh my, this is something to shine about. Jesus confirmed it when He said, "You are the light of the world. A city set on a hill cannot be hidden. Nor do people light a lamp and put it under a basket, but on a stand, and it gives light to all in the house. In the same way, let your light shine before others, so that they may see your good works and give glory to your Father who is in heaven" (Matthew 5:14-16).

Light up the neighborhood. Light up the world.

The Everlasting Light

We sing "O Little Town of Bethlehem" every year. It's a song sung to the city where our Jesus was born, and it includes the phrase:

"Yet in thy dark streets shineth

The everlasting Light;

The hopes and fears of all the years

Are met in thee tonight."

The everlasting Light that shone in Bethlehem is still shining. Our Father doesn't want us to pack away our thoughts of our Savior's coming like so many Christmas decorations. We're to shine Gospel-light-living through our streets and through our world.

So let's do it. Let's light it up in every season.

And if you'd specifically like to see it lit up come summer, head on over to my neighborhood. We'll leave the lights on.

Father, I celebrate You, my God who is Light. Jesus, Light of the World, I worship and glorify You. Holy Spirit who lights our way, I welcome You to guide me and influence every part of my heart, my life, my thoughts, my behavior—all of me. I am completely amazed at the beautiful way You have entered history in the most gloriously dramatic, bright and shining way. Your light has changed everything. By Your power, make me a light today. Use my life to shine Your love and truth into a dark world. Illuminate, I ask, in every way that would make You smile. In Jesus' name, amen.

Merry and Bright from Beth

Rhonda's got it right. I want to challenge how tinselly my thoughts are about Christ. Do I consistently shine all the hope at Christmas? Or do I pull Jesus out once a year to look over like some lingering, back-burner project? I want to celebrate the promise of who Christ is as much—and as shiny—as I can. I want my heart to be brighter than the brightest day in July. That's why waaay after Christmas I sometimes ... sorta ... still have lights on my boxwood bushes. And on my front porch. And the wrought iron fence ....

Chapter 24

Holiday Hush

Beth

*"'The root of Jesse will come, even he who arises to rule the
Gentiles; in him will the Gentiles hope.'
May the God of hope fill you with all joy and peace in
believing, so that by the power of the Holy Spirit you may
abound in hope" (Romans 15: 12-13).*

think it's important to take the time to enjoy this season. Can we try not to rush through so fast? Don't you think we're better off when we toss the hustle and bustle aside?

In fact, it's a smart coping skill to strive for slowness every day. Today, even. I know, because my daughter just greeted me at the door with, "Oh, Mom, the dog is out ... and your shirt is inside out. And backwards. You didn't go out like that did you?" *What?* Then she walked up the stairs to get her own self dressed the *right* way! *The nerve.*

I mean, if you're "correctly" dressed today—I want you to feel happy about it. Like celebrate you and pat your back where your tag is apparently living where no one can see it. You are one step ahead of me this holiday.

A pushed and scattered day is a train wreck waiting to happen, easy to crash and run off the tracks. Maybe I'm not alone as I get myself together in a holiday hurry. Lately I get stuck in this same ludicrous gear, somewhere between busier-than-normal and just-plain-not-normal. I'm like an under/over achiever zooming around with my tag hanging out. So many blessings go unnoticed in this seasonal rush. And that's just Christmas. Did you know there are other holidays to fit on the calendar, too?

For instance, there's a Clean Out Your Fridge Day on November 15th, a Have a Bad Day Day on November 19th. Then we have Cat Herders Day on December 15th. Who knew? And in *Fix Her Upper* language, this year has been a bit of a Demo Day, for sure. So how do we live free in this sometimes messy and inside-out, even backward space on the calendar? Because the pressure to dress right can be intense, for sure.

Unhurried

I'm not writing this chapter so you slow down and avoid dressing disasters. Or even take time to have a bad day intentionally and then clean out your fridge. (Wouldn't it make more sense for those holidays to hit the other way around?) But there is a day when you'll look back and marvel at all the good God has done.

It's the unnecessary things like hurry, worry, anxiety, and fear that encourage you to go faster. The world's expectations, they push hard, too. But my gosh, without your purposes headed in fresh directions, you might slow down but continue to live rushed. It's only when you take the time to pause in the unhurried presence of God that you'll notice: Repair and renewal for you were always part of His plan.

"And when his parents saw him, they were astonished. And his mother said to him, 'Son, why have you treated us so? Behold, your father and I have been searching for you in great distress.' And he said to them, 'Why were you looking for me? Did you not know that I must be in my Father's house?'" (Luke 2:48-49). The easier spirit of Christmas can be seen in a baby and our Lord coming as Christ. But also in the life Jesus lived while He was here.

Pace for Peace

Jesus' attentions are never in a hurry. These verses renew our focus and settle us into His pace for peace. We can't do all the things or be all the things to all people. We must be intentional with God. The *must* in verse 49 reveals our lives are best lived when settled into God's purpose. In His potential. In His company. Being in God's presence is what slows a hurried spirit down.

Anytime we pause in the presence of the Father there is good emphasized in our day. Have you ever noticed when you go to God seeking, you come away with His giving? Of love. Of help. Of goodness. Prayer emphasizes His progress—not ours. If we want to be deeply rooted in the transforming and renewing love of God, our time with Him should be real, not rushed.

Rushing through makes the simple seem hard. Take it from me, simply getting dressed can be a big, everything's-going-wrong deal. But not when we take the needed time to do it.

Catch Up with Confidence

Let's calmly catch up to the truth of God's steadiness. "God is in the midst of her; she shall not be moved; God will help her when the morning dawns" (Psalm 46:5). Girls, our God? He gets us! I love this verse and how it speaks of God's intentional love as He comforts the nation of Israel. Enemies threatened from every side while the secure love of the Lord steadied His people. His amazing love hasn't changed—sometimes it's only our hurry-scurry perspective that's moved. We meet His possibility when we meet Him. Early is good. Before we get up and dressed, even better.

This Christmas has a chance to be different, while the miracle that Jesus came stays the same. After all, Scripture tells us God's favor rests on us. As His angels prayed and praised, saying, "Glory to God in the highest heaven, and on earth peace to those on whom his favor rests" (Luke 2:14 NIV). At Christmas. Anytime. Prayer gives us unhurried-harmony in this sometimes messy and unbalanced life we live.

Not just any prayer though—we can pray with miraculous requests. We don't tend to ask for the miraculous and large when we see a small God. When I think about the concept of asking God for big joy, big refreshment, or major heart repair, I remember something singer songwriter Babbie Mason once said to me. "Beth, we serve a big God. You're asking too small! Pray big. God is miraculous in blessing and answers perfectly. So pray Bigger!" Since then, I've learned to ask expectantly while God catches me up to His confidence. God knows the power in Him perfects the process in me. A longer look at the Christmas story and we know God answers. We're in the quick days of Christmas, let's hang on.

Holiday Hush

In the last few days of wonder, I can fall short. A calmer holiday starts when I make God my go-to. My own soul-potential? A complete DIY disaster, but not with God in the renovation process.

Over and over we watch as Jesus steps away from the crowds. Walks off quietly to pray. Then, at the Sea of Galilee, He walks on water. Before every emphasis in His ministry, there was intentional slow time with His Father. Jesus declares, "Believe me that I am in the Father and the Father is in me" (John 14:11a). What a great reminder that when we stop and take notice, the Spirit of God is new in us every day.

So if you've been Christmasing nonstop, and you're determined to get every last drop of the season in, watching snowflakes may seem like a severe stop. It's not. Give yourself a break and escape the holiday rush. It's in this stalled time you'll sense the holiday hush. Take it from me. As I change my shirt. Inside-right. And frontwards. But also take it from me—it's way better than cleaning out the fridge.

Father, it's such soul relief to know that You call us to walk with You. Not to sprint ahead or lag behind. But ... with You." It's a fierce, battle-worthy charge. And because I could use some calm relief today—I have this hope: You wait for me! Thank You for this day and all the hope that it holds. Be glorified, Lord, I pray. In Your steadfast name. Amen.

Thrill of Hope with Rhonda

Inside-out and backwards. Been there. I think we should get points when our shirts are not upside-down. I don't think either one of us have done that one, have we, Beth? Not yet anyway.

Wild, hurry-hurry-rush days happen to all of us. What I want to hang onto, in Beth's words, is "the unhurried presence of God." I want to come humbly to that place referred to in this chapter, a place of becoming deeply rooted in the transforming and renewing love of God. It's a glorious marvel that He waits for me there. Patiently. And that I can rest there. Fully. Even with my shirt tag on the outside.

Chapter 25

Ho Ho Huh?

Rhonda and Beth

Raise your hand if you DIY your own Christmas cards. OK, now put your hands back down as we, Rhonda and Beth, slink quietly away in disgrace. Cutesy photo of the fam? That's a nope over here. The dog in a Santa hat? Still no. We have yet to put a single elf suit on a cat this entire season.

Most Christmases, the two of us get utterly overwhelmed simply looking at the Christmas card list. Has that ever happened to you? (You hand-raisers from the first paragraph have permission to sit in judgment throughout the next several paragraphs.) Do-it-yourselfer or don't-do-it-yourselfer, have you ever had your Christmas joy grinched right out of you at the thought of all that looming Christmas card shuffling? It's like all the air gets sucked out of your "ho ho ho."

It doesn't help that some of us start that card shuffle at a time in the season that's way too close to "too late." Then we pull a couple of ridiculous all-nighters, trying to address, stamp, sign, seal, deliver—all in peregrine falcon style. Swoop.

Our Lips Are Sealed

One of the worst happenings is when you finally make it to bed in the wee hours of the morning after one of those all-night card parties and then have trouble sleeping because of the lingering taste of envelope glue. Gross. No wait, worse than that is when you wake up the next morning and find your tongue is pasted to the roof of your mouth. No matter what he licks, bet that never happens to your average bird of prey.

We've been striving to hit the truth from all directions through this book, that our joy is only grinched out of our season when we allow it to be. We allow it when we get overwhelmed with the small stuff or distracted by all the shinies of the season. We allow it when our focus lands on the temporary and we miss what matters. We allow it when we get wrapped up in the wrappings and trappings of a birthday party, all the while missing the One with the birthday, the true Guest of Honor.

The Guest of Honor, our Jesus, is the most precious, the most inestimably valuable, the most life-changing gift that's ever been given. God the Creator took on flesh and humbly came to Earth, all so that each of us might find closeness with Him. An eternal relationship. Christmas is God sending us a living Christmas card of grace. His coming is a declaration to the world that He loves us, and that we are lost without Him.

The Lord completed the work of salvation at the Cross and proved it by the resurrection. John clues us into that loving work of salvation. "For God so [greatly] loved and dearly prized the world, that He [even] gave His [One and] only begotten Son, so that whoever believes and trust in Him [as Savior] shall not perish, but have eternal life. For God did not send the Son into the world to judge and condemn the world [that is, to initiate the final judgment of the world], but that the world might be saved through Him" (John 3:16-17 AMP).

Oh, This Plan

What a love! What a redemption plan! It was God's plan long before the first Christmas. Isaiah prophesied, "But he was pierced for our transgressions; he was crushed for our iniquities; upon him was the chastisement that brought us peace, and with his wounds we are healed. All we like sheep have gone astray; we have turned—every one—to his own way; and the Lord has laid on him the iniquity of us all" (Isaiah 53:5-6).

Our sin—our legit disgrace. We have a God who is holy beyond what our finite minds can comprehend. In His holiness, He can't have fellowship with sin. But we've, "every one" Isaiah says, turned our own way. Done our own thing. Gone in a heart direction that's completely the opposite of God's way. Without a perfect, sinless Savior to pay for our sin, we're all doomed to an eternity separated from our holy God.

Yet, Christmas. God played the Grace card. The card beyond all cards. In His mercy He has made new life available to us in His New Covenant—signed, sealed, delivered by and through the blood of Jesus Christ. Jesus paid our sin debt, and the love of a holy God became something oh so real for each of us. Available. Experienceable. Transformational.

The Grace card is addressed to you, friends. It's personal.

All-In This Christmas

If you've never become an all-in follower of the Christ of Christmas, there could not be a better time. You can love your God and settle your eternity—no matter where you are, what you're doing, where you've been, what you've done. We invite you to pray something like this:

> *Father, I know I've broken Your laws and chosen my own way instead of Yours. I've sinned against You. Holy God, thank You for sending Jesus, Your only Son, to pay for my sin with His own blood. Please forgive me by that blood, I ask. I believe that Jesus died for me and rose again, conquering sin and death once and for all. I trust You right now to cleanse my every sin, to make me clean and new. Thank You for loving me. I give*

my life and my all to You. Empower me to serve You with
everything I have and everything I am, with every day You give
me, from this moment forward. May my life bring glory to You.
Thank You for saving me. In Jesus' Name, Amen."

If you just prayed that kind of prayer for the first time, your destiny has changed—forever and in every way for the better. Your life, changed. Your heart, changed! You've been set free from sin and its penalty, and you now have the Spirit of God living and working inside you, helping you to know Him better, and helping you fulfill everything you were created for. It's the most satisfying, dreams-coming-true kind of life.

Paul said, "In Him we have redemption [that is, our deliverance and salvation] through His blood, [which paid the penalty for our sin and resulted in] the forgiveness and complete pardon of our sin, in accordance with the riches of His grace which He lavished on us" (Ephesians 1:7-8a AMP).

Living Out the Christmas Joy

Whether you're a new follower, or you've been living the life of faith for decades, recognizing and remembering that the celebration of the birth of Christ is the celebration of our redemption. Nothing puts the joy in Christmas—or life—like loving and following the Christ. He is the one who makes joy possible, and who keeps the "ho ho ho" fully resonating in our hearts.

So from the bottom of our fix-her-upper hearts, we wish you all the merriest of Christmases. May each of you experience all the magnificent wonders of Christ the King as you journey the season with Him.

Joy to the world, the Lord is come!

Acknowledgments

Oh how we love and appreciate our husbands. Jerry Duewel and Richie Rhea continue to be the absolute best at being the absolute best. We love acknowledging them right here—with nods of huge thanks and big kisses on top—for support and encouragement far beyond the call of duty. Thank you both for all you do.

More thank yous to our fams, who've invested prayer and encouragement and who are all the cutest. Appreciation to the Duewel team: Brittany, John, Brooklyn, Josh, Amber and Branson. And to the Rhea team: Andy, Amber, Asa, Amos, Jordan, Camille, Kaley, Allie, Derek, Emerson, Oswyn, August, Daniel, Olivia, and Ainsley. We love and appreciate you, our sweet, sweet families.

Huge thanks to our ministry friends, the team at Bold Vision Books, especially to George Porter and Karen Porter. We can't say enough good things about your lovely hearts for ministry. And to Amber Weigand-Buckley for creative, amazing design work and all kinds of marketing and ministry helps. What would we do without our Amber W-B #BAREFACEDCREATIVE?

A special, over-animated nod—like, a ridiculously over-the-top, dramatic head bob—to Kaley Rhea. We're forever indebted for the generous load of creativity, input, edits—the works.

As always, so much thanks—so very much—to Rhonda's and Beth's prayer teams. The prayer investment of these godly women makes all the ministry difference.

Pamela Harty, friend and agent—and to all the wonderful people at The Knight Agency—we are so grateful for your "ministry of details." Thank you for taking care of all those deets so that we can focus on the rest.

Sincere nods of appreciation to the Advanced Writers and Speakers Association for shared knowledge, prayers, encouragement, connection, and counsel.

Thank you, our sweet church fams, Rhonda's at NorthRoad Community Church and Beth's at Grace Church. Your prayers and support mean so much.

Ever and always, our deepest debt of gratitude belongs to our Jesus. We celebrate Your birth with full hearts from the first chapter of this book to the last. We celebrate You all year long. Every day. Every way. Thank You, Savior, for Your coming, and for your permanent fix of our souls. You are our JOY.

MEET RHONDA AND BETH

Beth Duewel is a writer, speaker, and blogger at fix-her-upper.
com. Coauthor of the Fix-Her-Upper Book series, she also is a regular
contributor to Christian Broadcasting Network and Arise Daily
Devotions. Beth lives in Ashland, Ohio, where she finds joy in the
everyday with husband, Jerry. She is mom to three grown children
and Nana to one spoiled grandbabe. Oh. What. Fun!

Rhonda Rhea is an award-winning humor columnist for
great magazines such as *HomeLife, Leading Hearts, The Pathway,*
and many more. She leans heavily into her *Fix-Her-Upper*-ness
and says she loves co-authoring the series with Beth Duewel. She is
the author of 19 books, including the popular romantic comedies
co-authored with her daughter, Kaley Rhea, *Off-Script & Over-
Caffeinated and Turtles in the Road* (both winning multiple major
awards, one a Golden Scroll winner and one a Christy Award finalist).
Rhonda also teams up with Kaley and Monica Schmelter for the
Messy to Meaningful books and TV projects and she co-authored

Unruffled: Thriving in Chaos with Edie Melson as well. She speaks at conferences and events from coast to coast, serves on many boards and committees, and stays busy as a publishing consultant. Rhonda says you can find her living near St. Louis drinking too much coffee and snort-laughing with her pastor/husband, Richie Rhea, their five grown children, and a growing collection of the most exceptional grandbabies.

Made in USA - Kendallville, IN
1202695_9781946708557
12.01.2020 1033